BACK IN THE DAY

BACK IN THE DAY

Growing Up in the Fifties:
I Still Haven't Met a Train I Didn't Like

LOU PALUMBO

WINDY CITY
PUBLISHERS

BACK IN THE DAY
Growing Up in the Fifties:
I Still Haven't Met a Train I Didn't Like

Windy City Publishers
2118 Plum Grove Rd., #349
Rolling Meadows, IL 60008
www.windycitypublishers.com

Published in the United States of America

ISBN-13:
978-1-941478-63-9

Library of Congress Control Number:
2018937985

Cover Photo Credits:
Front Cover: Lou at home with grandson Chris Conti, who is the Webmaster for The Underground Railroad Shoppe website. Both are avid Dodger fans. Photo taken by Kellyanne Conti, Lou's granddaughter. Photo edited and submitted by Todd Palumbo, Lou's son.

Back Cover: File photo of Red 1955 Ford Thunderbird, exactly like the T-Bird owned by Lou's sister Anarose. Photo edited and submitted by Todd Palumbo.

WINDY CITY PUBLISHERS
CHICAGO

To my parents and sisters who guided this "little guy"
through those wonderful years of the fifties with
a great family life for which I am most thankful.

To all of my buddies from the Pearson street neighborhood and Dean Park,
the fun and adventures that we had made this book possible .
I will never forget them.

To all of my classmates and the sisters of St. Vitus School
for eight years in the 1950s. Especially to my "gang"
(you know who you are), that we lived and learned with
great memories that we will always remember.

CONTENTS

PART 1:
Growing Up in the Fifties

Family and Life in the Neighborhood

Downtown and All Around

Fun with My Friends

Growing Up and Getting Older

PART 2:
I Still Haven't Met a Train I Didn't Like

Essays from 2014

Essays from 2015

Essays from 2016

Essays from 2017

Essays from 2018

FOREWORD

ARE YOU READY? PACK A peanut butter and jelly sandwich, lace up your P.F. Flyers, and prepare to travel back to the wonderful years of the 1950s. The book you are holding is about to transform itself into a time machine, one sure to take you from your living room or deck to a small town in western Pennsylvania decades ago.

A time machine? Do I mean a contraption invented by H.G. Wells or the jazzed-up DeLorean assembled by Doc Brown in the movie *Back to the Future*?

Not at all. This time machine is smaller, quieter, and a lot cheaper. It is this book filled with nearly 50 warm and delightful chapters, recalling what it was like to grow up in an Italian family in the 15 years after the end of World War II.

Lou Palumbo, my good friend and fellow toy train enthusiast and rock music lover, has done it again. One of the great storytellers of our time, he seems to have remembered everything about coming of age in a little city located near Pittsburgh. And can Lou tell a tale! Reading his vignettes carries you back with him to a time and place so different from our America in the early 21st century.

When Lou escorts you to New Castle during the Eisenhower years, you do more than just feel comfortable and nostalgic. You become one of Lou's pals.

Hanging around with Lou when he was a kid meant smelling the food cooking in Mrs. Palumbo's kitchen. You'll munch popcorn while watching on the movie screen Roy Rogers or James Dean. You'll grab your sled after a snowstorm or jump into a creek on an August afternoon after playing baseball all morning.

Best of all, you're about to get to know better a truly terrific gentleman. What more can I say about Lou, whose column in *Classic Toy Trains* I have been editing for more than 10 years (we've collected the latest ones for this new book)?

Let me share my own story, one I think reveals so much about Lou. When finishing this book, I asked Lou if he wanted to write about the nicknames boys typically gave each other back when we were growing up. He declined after considering that certain names were a bit derogatory ("Shorty" or "Turtle").

Then I asked Lou if he had had a nickname. "Sure," he replied in his usual matter-of-fact tone. "Everybody called me 'Big Lou.' Not that I was the tallest or the toughest kid in our neighborhood. But because my pals seemed to follow me."

Makes sense! As anyone who has ever spent time with Lou can attest, he has the rare qualities of a natural leader. He speaks honestly yet never harshly. Lou treats people fairly and expects a lot from them, while he has the habit of giving of himself. You easily understand why kids on the basketball court, in classrooms, or strolling downtown always paid attention to what he said and did.

So let's climb into Big Lou's time machine and crank the dials to take us about 65 years in the past. A time when rock 'n' roll was new, the Dodgers were still playing in Brooklyn, and department stores featured electric trains in their windows at Christmas. A time when television was a novelty, and listening to your grandparents relate how they had immigrated to America was routine.

A grand time will be had by everyone who hears Lou's stories. In fact, I'll bet that his tales will cause you to remember your own and the best parts of your growing up. If Lou can inspire your memories, you can bet he will be very proud.

~Roger Carp
Senior Editor
Classic Toy Trains Magazine

ACKNOWLEDGMENTS

Roger Carp, Senior Editor *Classic Toy Trains* Magazine
To my good friend, editor, and train mentor. The inspiration for many of my
ideas for the monthly columns and stories in CTT.
Many thanks, Roger, for now and years to come.

Carl Swanson, Editor of *Classic Toy Trains* Magazine,
the number one toy train magazine in the world.
We often talk about the hobby and exchange thoughts new ideas.
Again Carl helped to transfer the magazine columns to Part 2 of this book.
Thanks, Carl.

Bob Keller, Associate Editor of *Classic Toy Trains* Magazine.
Bob's continued support of all of my projects and sharing thoughts
on new products in the hobby.
Thanks, Bob, from your favorite model train raconteur.

Tom McComas, Owner and Producer T.M. books and Videos
Mike Wolf, President, CEO of M.T.H. Trains
Ken Bianco, Owner of Trainworld, Brooklyn, New York
Len Carparelli, Owner of L&L Model Train Restoration Co.
Conversations and regular contact with these long-time friends help me keep
in touch with the pulse of the model train hobby. Thanks, guys.

Finally, The Underground Railroad Shoppe production crew:
Chris Conti, Webmaster and Production.
Richard L. Conti, Production and Typing
Brandon Conti, Production and Typing
Gavyn Hansotte, Typing
Bill Dunkle, Photographs
Joshua Urban, Typing
Without these guys, no book, no columns.
Thanks!

INTRODUCTION

I HAVE BEEN WRITING A monthly column for *Classic Toy Trains* magazine for more than ten years. Many of my columns refer to the enthusiasm of collecting toy trains during the decade of 1950. Two phrases that I use often when writing about the times of 1950s are "Back in the day" and "Old school." I like these phrases because they soften the term in the "olden days." It's usually a time point referring to former years.

The other phrase, "Old school," softens any reference of the ways things used to be done and are still useful. These phrases hit me in my comfort zone when I'm remembering the way things used to be. This book was written as a comfort food of the mind, a mental aspirin for days that you don't have to work so hard to feel good.

I put together many short stories of how things were for this "little guy" growing up in the 1950s. All the events occurred from 1950 until 1960 when I was 16 years old. There are millions of other kids that grew up during these years. These are some of the things that happened to make us the great generation of "baby boomers".

As a bonus, I have included four years of monthly columns that were not covered in my first book, *I Never Met a Train I Didn't Like*.

So sit back, read and enjoy these stories and take a "mental aspirin" as you go "Back in the Day."

~Lou Palumbo
April 2018

PART 1:
Growing Up in the Fifties

FAMILY AND LIFE
IN THE NEIGHBORHOOD

COMING TO AMERICA

MY FATHER'S FAMILY CAME TO America from the Province of Caserta in Italy in the late 1890s. Look on a map and you'll find Caserta north of Naples in the southern part of the country. People were leaving Italy in the late 19th century to escape the effects of a terrible depression. People referred to the situation then as "morte fama" which translates as "the worst kind of death," meaning death by starvation.

Due to the limited number of people allowed to immigrate to America, many had to come to the country illegally. Among them were individuals in a group known as the "Black Hand" ("mana nero" in Italian). The Black Hand went to Italy in search of able-bodied men. They gathered them and then sent them illegally to America. Once in the United States, the Illegal immigrants were given jobs at sites controlled by the Black Hand. Extorting money from the poor immigrants came next for the merciless Black Hand.

Hillsville, Pennsylvania, was known as a place where the Black Hand existed. There were many limestone quarries in Hillsville, and the immigrants worked at those quarries while living in company houses. The meager wages paid the men ended up being even worse after the Black Hand had taken their cut. Such was life in America for many thousands of helpless migrants.

My grandparents, Luigi and Angela Rosa Palumbo, had traveled from Italy and came to Hillsville. There, on October 8, 1900, my father was born. He was named Francesco Antonio Palumbo. He had six sisters. My father and his family soon moved from Hillsville to another small town in the western part of Pennsylvania known as Mahoningtown. My grandfather went to work there for the Pennsylvania Railroad. My mother was born in Naples, Italy, in 1910 to Raphaelle and Olympia Morella. The family immigrated to America in 1914 and settled in New Castle, Pennsylvania, not too far from Mahoningtown.

In those days, most people who came from Italy to America wanted to live near relatives or friends who were Italian. They did this because of the language barrier and so helped each other get "Americanized." Feeling at home in America was so important to Italian immigrants. That was the reason my parents never taught my sisters or me to speak Italian. They were afraid we would be ridiculed in school. Looking back, I think my parents were mistaken. We should have been taught to speak both Italian and English fluently. We were robbed of having a second language growing up.

My mother was the oldest of nine children. She had to quit school while in junior high to help her mother with her younger siblings. Her dad, meanwhile, worked for the Pennsylvania Railroad. Mom always regretted having to quit school, but there really was no choice. My mother's parents lived next door to us. They had a large hillside lot resembling their yard in Italy and used it to help feed their family. My grandparents had a big garden with many fruit trees and a grapevine (my grandfather made his own wine every year). They also kept chickens and two goats.

Dad and Mom married in 1927. Little did they know the Great Depression was on the horizon, rocking the national economy when the stock market crashed in October of 1929. The Depression lasted for 10 years.

Over the first dozen years my parents were married, they had three daughters, Anarose, Olivia, and Lucille. Times were hard for everyone, but Dad seemed to manage. In later years I understood why my parents were always so careful with their money. Mom never failed to refer to the desperate days of the Depression. My mother did not believe in wasting anything and would not spend money on "foolish things." No problem, because we always seemed to have what we needed. If we didn't have it, we didn't need it.

We were a very happy family. I always said, "I never knew we were poor until someone told me." The Great Depression ended around 1940. I was born four years later. The glorious 1950s were right around the corner.

STAY-AT-HOME MOM

SOME OF MY EARLIEST MEMORIES were those of my life during my preschool years. Let me share a few with you, so you can get to know me better.

I was born on December 20, 1944. That turned out to be twelve days before New Year's Day of 1945, which has become the official designation of the "baby boom" generation (1945-65).

My father, Frank, and my mother, Josephine, already had three daughters by the time I was born. My older sisters were 10, 14, and 16 when I arrived. My parents also had had a son 17 years before in 1927. Sadly, he died at four months of pneumonia. His name was Louis, and they would give it to me. My parents wanted to honor the Italian tradition of naming the first male child after his father. Therefore, it was important to my family to pass that name, Louis, down to me.

1951 | My family, "mia famiglia" | Dad, Mom, and sisters, Anarose, Olivia, Lucille, and "the little king"

3

On that cold December day in 1944, the Palumbo family received what I can modestly say everyone agreed was the best gift ever. No coincidence I was born five days before Christmas.

My father was 44 years old at the time of my birth. I do not have to tell you how proud he was to have his own little boy.

Mom was 10 years younger than my dad. She was the eldest of nine children and had left school while in junior high to help her mother raise their family. Mom never let her lack of formal education affect her knowledge of worldly things. She was a remarkable woman and taught me much during my preschool years.

In those days, most mothers did not work outside the home. Instead, they stayed at home to raise children. They were called housewives.

Maybe some people consider this term a bit degrading for women, although I don't know why. No one did back when I was growing up. Just the opposite: being a housewife was acceptable and honorable.

What else can I tell you about my mother? She never learned to drive a car, so we walked everywhere we had to go during the day.

Our family had a small electric refrigerator at home. Before that, as I can vaguely recall from my earliest days, we had what was called an icebox. An icebox was exactly what you think. A small cabinet held a block of ice in the bottom shelf that kept cold all the food stored there. We soon got the electric refrigerator.

Daily shopping trips to town were necessary to buy groceries for Mom to turn into nourishing and filling meals. I spent most of my time during those days with her. She had a wealth of information she enjoyed sharing with her only son.

For our family and so many others in postwar America, the main source of information about the outside world was the daily newspaper. At the same time, radio kept us in touch with world news and local happenings.

Radio was also a source of wonderful entertainment. I remember listening to various "kids" programs starring Gene Autry and Roy Rogers.

Many other popular shows for children usually played between 4 and 5 o'clock.

I enjoyed accompanying Mom on visits to neighbors and relatives living nearby. Our visits were always a lot of fun, as I usually spent time playing with other kids or my cousins while Mom talked and caught up on what was new.

I never realized until much later how simple and valuable those days were and how much I learned from that wonderful woman. Mom was so sharp when it came to judging people. That wasn't all. Mom ran our home with great efficiency. Later in life, she managed the small grocery store my family owned.

Mom's skills with people were great. Maybe that's where I learned how to treat the customers and other folks who drop by my toy train store.

The most valuable lesson I picked up from Mom was to always look for the best in people. She said, "If you can't say something good about a person, then make something up."

DAD THE RAILROADER

MY EARLY MEMORIES OF DAD were that he was a very hardworking, kind, and proud person. Nearly every morning during my preschool years started with breakfast with Dad. He would be up at 5 o'clock to get ready to go to work at the Pennsylvania Railroad car shop located in our hometown in western Pennsylvania.

When I heard Dad getting up, I would rush to join him for a small breakfast that usually included toast and coffee. Dad would give me a little coffee in a bowl with a lot of milk and sugar. Also, a handful of oyster crackers floated in the bowl with the sweetened coffee. It was great to talk with Dad and spend a little time each morning before he left for work while it was still dark outside.

Mom prepared lunch for my father. It usually included sandwiches made from the previous day's supper. She packed the sandwiches in waxed paper and added fruit wrapped with newspaper shaped like a box tied with string. I remember seeing some of the oil from the fried pepper sandwiches marking the outside of the paper.

Dad left, gripping carefully the square package holding his lunch. Then I went back to bed. By the way, I thought that was the way lunches were packed until I saw kids with brown paper bags and steel lunch boxes after I started school.

Sometimes, Dad would take me to the Pennsy car shop on Saturday mornings. That was a great thrill to me. We walked around the yard, and Dad showed me the storage shanty, where he kept all the supplies used on the freight trains ready to leave.

At that time, Dad's job involved inspecting each freight train about to leave his yard. He was called a car inspector. Saturday morning visits usually ended with a ride on a switcher engine around the yard. Dad's buddies gave me the trip, a practice I am sure would be illegal now. These visits with Dad were highlights of my younger days. I guess they represented the start of my love for trains and eventually my love for toy and model trains.

Later, in my preteen years, I accompanied Dad when he was called out at night to expect an outgoing train due to leave early the next morning. Did I mind going out late at night to help? Not at all! I felt so special walking alongside Dad as he inspected each boxcar, gondola, hopper, and other types on those long trains. He applied oil to any car axle needing it.

I held a flashlight as Dad inspected the freight car. If he found anything irregular, he tagged the car so it was removed from the train before the trip. I loved to inspect each caboose, because each of them was equipped with a lot of neat stuff. A potbelly stove was on each caboose. Sometimes Dad and I started a fire in the stove to make the caboose warm for the fellows on the next shift.

Dad and I also checked the leather cushions that were supplied. I liked to climb up to the cupola, where I could view the entire train.

I often wondered why Dad never worked as an engineer or a conductor on a regular train route. Later I was told that most of the men who worked at the car shop were immigrants. Jobs there were hard and demanding, especially in the foundry. Immigrants were given that work and not assigned to the better jobs on the trains.

Dad worked at the local car shop the entire time of his employment at the Pennsylvania Railroad. During those 40 years there, he did every kind of job asked of him, no matter how grueling.

Circumstances changed later, thanks to the growth of employee unions during the late 1940s. Then jobs were given out by seniority and the ability to do a specific job, Men were not evaluated by the color of their skin or their nationality.

THE BUICK

MY DAD OWNED A 1948 torpedo-back two-door Buick Roadmaster he bought used in 1950. The car, which looked brand new when he brought it home, came painted two-tone gray. Dad kept the Buick in an old single-car garage behind our house. He stated that he drove it only for weddings, funerals, and an occasional Sunday drive to visit relatives living out of town. Otherwise, he drove an old panel truck or pickup back and forth to work.

I often sat in the Buick as it rested in the garage and pretended I was driving on a long trip. Needless to say, my buddies and I were not permitted to be in the car. We went there only when Dad was at work, as I knew where he hid the key. He always knew when I was in the car and hollered at me when he got home.

ITALIAN WEDDINGS

ALL WEDDINGS ARE WONDERFUL, BUT there is nothing like an Italian one, especially the way they were done in the 1950s. I was fortunate enough to be a part of two of them, experienced when my older sisters got married in the mid-1950s.

Preparation for the wedding started in earnest about a week before the day of the festivities. That was when women began making the cookies. My mother rounded up a bunch of my aunts and other women to come to our house every day for a week and make cookies. I loved the smell of the house during the time not to mention the pleasure of tasting the freshly baked goodies.

Italian cookies have the distinctive smell of anise as well as all the other ingredients. The cookies were baked and placed in clean wicker bushels lined with white linen and waxed paper. They were stored in an unused bedroom kept locked until the wedding day.

An Italian wedding lasted an entire day. It started with a breakfast typically held at a local hall. The breakfast was smaller than the lunch that followed the wedding mass held mid-morning. The mass was conducted at St. Vitus church and usually ended by noon. At the end of the mass the bride and groom came out of the church and were showered by rice and something special called "coombits."

For those of you who have never heard of "coombits," they were brightly colored candy-coated almonds mixed with the rice and loose change. Then they were thrown on the bride and groom for good luck. It was a wonder more wedding couples were not injured with this good luck shower. Little children scrambled on the ground to retrieve the candy and money. Birds got the rice. It was a lot of fun.

The wedding party and close friends would then go to a local hall or restaurant where lunch was served. It was at one of these events I got my first taste of that culinary delight the world knows as Italian Wedding

Soup. What we referred to as "Wedding Soup" consisted of small meat-balls, chunks of boiled chicken, and fresh greens, all cooked in a delicious chicken broth. This still is one of my favorite soups.

Besides the Weddings Soup, we generally had ravioli, " Braciole", meatballs, and sausage in tomato sauce. Can't leave out the different fresh fruits and salads, along with the traditional Italian pastries.

After lunch, everyone usually retreated to their home or a guest home if they were from out of town. They had to get ready for the big reception held in the evening. It included all the friends and relatives of the bride and groom. Many people were usually invited to attend the reception. By today's standards the wedding receptions were relatively simple because people could not afford to feed that many people invited to the receptions nowadays.

The wedding reception was usually held in a large hall. The bridal table was situated in a spot where everyone could come to the reception and be greeted by the bride, groom, and their parents in front of a large table where the bridal party sat. The attendees would congratulate the bride and groom and give them an envelope to be put in a box and guarded by a family member. After every congratulation, the men drank shots of whiskey. It didn't take long for some of the guys to get loaded.

The hall was surrounded by three or four rows of chairs facing the dance floor in a large circle. The band was usually on the stage at one end of the hall. The music started, and everyone danced.

During the evening, delicious ham and Italian hot ham sandwiches wrapped in waxed paper bags were passed out to everyone. Ladies would follow the sandwiches with trays of the homemade cookies. All the drinks, including coffee and soda pop, were self-served at the bar.

There was always a large gathering of men around the bar, usually situated in a room off the main ballroom. That room grew louder and louder as the men talked and hollered while drinking beer. They seemed to be having a lot of fun, but once in a while a fight broke out that had to be settled by cooler heads.

1952 | I was the ring bearer for my sister Olivia's wedding

The wedding reception usually started around seven and ended by midnight. Before the close, often around 9 o'clock, the cake march was orchestrated on the dance floor. It featured the entire wedding party. The march preceded the cutting of the wedding cake. After the bride and groom indulged in their pieces of cake, the rest of the huge wedding cake was sliced into pieces served on napkins by ladies to the entire hall.

The cutting of the cake was followed by a traditional bridal dance that always concluded with the father of the bride and the bride dancing to the tune of "Daddy's Little Girl." You can guess how fast everyone was soon crying. Go figure.

The band played the rest of the night and usually included an Italian dance called the "Tarantella." By that time everyone was feeling pretty good. The place got loud, and the louder the band played the louder people talked. Weddings gave all of us a chance to see many of our friends and relatives from out of town. Families were bound together by these occasions. We don't seem to have this today.

THE CORNER STORE

IN 1952, MY PARENTS BOUGHT a corner grocery store from my aunt and uncle after they had moved to another town. The store was in a small brick building attached to their home, which my mom and dad also purchased at that time. Access to the store from the house was gained through a door in the cellar of the house.

In the 1950s, there seemed to be a small family-owned grocery store on every corner. Most housewives did not have transportation, so they needed to do their shopping each day at a market close enough for them to walk to. My family owned Palumbo's Grocery Store until my parents closed it in the early 1970s. By that time, there were several supermarkets in town and many women were working outside the home and driving cars. Things had really changed.

1958 | Palumbo corner grocery store

Some of my best childhood memories originated at my family's grocery store. Mom managed it while Dad went to work on the railroad. I was enlisted to help at the store from the day Mom and Dad took over. Starting at the age of eight, I carried boxes and stocked shelves. As I grew older, I began to wait on customers.

There always was something happening in the store. We stayed open until 8 or 9 each night. I learned a lot about people and politics while listening to the conversations held by the adults who visited the store.

Palumbo's Grocery Store carried lots of fresh produce and vegetables. Cold cuts and imported Italian cheeses were favorites. We sliced each order individually and sold it by the pound. Mom baked her own pizza every day. She would cut them in square pieces and put them in wax paper bags. The store would smell great while she was making pizza. Her pizza was great everyone loved it.

However, the overall favorite seller was my dad's homemade Italian sausage. To this day I have never had any better. Just ask around our town, and you'll be told Mr. Palumbo had the best Italian sausage in the city.

We opened on Sunday morning at 9 o'clock after the 7 o'clock mass at our Catholic church ended. Mom prepared the sauce for our Sunday dinner in the kitchen in a room behind the store. People came in after mass and lined up to buy sausage for their Sunday dinner.

Around noon on Sundays, we generally closed the store for the day and had dinner with our family in the main kitchen in our home. That was always a must-be-there event by my mother's rule.

The sausage business was best during the fall and winter months. During the holiday season, Dad and I made hundreds of pounds of sausage that sold out every day. I learned every detail about making Italian sausage and still make it today. I know Dad's recipe for that delicacy. If I told it to anybody, I would have to see that they were no longer with us.

Dad used only the best pork butts, which is really the shoulder and not what you might think. And he never, ever put any filler in his sausage.

During the holiday seasons, we decorated the store with colorful lights and had many traditional seasonal foods and meats at that time. The store smelled wonderful at Christmastime. Everybody seemed to be in a good mood during the season.

Summer was also neat to be in the store. My buddies hung out on a stoop next to the storefront. We sat on a cement ledge facing the street.

We stayed there till late, watching the cars and people go by. All the guys bought soda pops and food to consume on those hot summer nights. Naturally, we cleaned up. Dad made sure of that, or he would not have let us come back.

Mom, as I mentioned before, had to quit school after junior high. She was the oldest daughter and had to help her mother with her eight younger brothers and sisters.

All the same, Mom was very smart and had a lot of wisdom. She managed that small store herself as long as it was open. She did all the ordering and dealt with salesmen like a real professional. I always admired her for that.

1954 | Lou in corner store with dad and mom

THE NEIGHBORHOOD

OUR TOWN WAS LIKE MOST small cities in America in the 1950s. Towns were built near rivers and railroads, which was the main mode of transportation at the beginning of the 20th century. Industrial areas and commercial districts were usually located around the rivers and railroads. The residential areas surrounded the business areas on all sides.

Neighborhoods were made up of wooden frame two-story houses built on small lots and close together on each street. Each house had a small front and back yard. Some areas had row houses: residences connected to each other. There were hardly any row houses in the town where I grew up.

We lived on Pearson street. Most of the people in our neighborhood were of Italian descent. They were first-generation immigrants who had arrived in this country in the early 1900s. They lived near other Italian immigrants who already were American citizens. The language barrier helped people of similar nationalities communicate. They gradually learned to speak English.

Most of the people on our street had small gardens in their back yards. Many of them had grape arbors with a picnic table placed under the arbor. Men congregated under their arbors during good weather and passed the time while drinking their homemade wine. This practice had been carried to America by their parents from Italy.

The neighborhoods were very clean, and there was no crime. I don't think any people felt a need to lock their doors. Our backdoor was locked by a skeleton key that could be easily purchased at any five-and-dime store.

There were many young boys and girls in every neighborhood in the 1950s. They usually hung around in groups and walked to school together. Later in the evening they played games until the streetlights went on. Then everyone knew it was time to go home.

Our neighborhood was peaceful, and many of the houses had comfortable front porches where people sat on the warm summer evenings. Sometimes, people spoke to each other as they sat on their porches. It was not uncommon to hear voices communicating to each other at night.

Walking down the street you could hear radios being played. Popular music and baseball games were heard in the distance during those warm summer nights in the 1950s.

1952 | Lou and buddy Jackie Long
practicing their western fast draw

NEIGHBORHOOD VISITORS

DURING THE LATE 1940S AND early '50s, our neighborhood had many vendors and other people who regularly visited. Mothers were usually home, so the vendors would come daily to try to sell their goods and services.

Let's start with the "produce man." A frequent visitor in the area, he drove a large truck with open sides so everyone could see all of his fruits and vegetables. The produce man parked on various streets, and women gathered around to purchase his fresh fruits and vegetables.

The produce man stood at the back of his truck. I remember the large hanging scale he used to weigh the oranges, potatoes, and more. I always hung around the truck, waiting to be thrown a fresh peach or a banana as a free sample. We called these fellows "hucksters." They always put on a good show when they traveled through the neighborhoods.

Another fellow who visited the neighborhood was known as the "scissors man." He pushed a small cart, and all the ladies would go out to get their knives and scissors sharpened. The scissors man sharpened tools with a grinding wheel mounted on his cart and operated with a foot petal. I thought that was neat and imagined I might like to be a scissors man when I grew up. It seemed like a sharp job, so to speak! You could buy a new knife or a pair of scissors from the scissors man, among other kinds of tools. He also sold handmade, high-quality leather goods: purses, wallets, and other small items. You can't get stuff like that today. The scissors man fixed my baseball glove when it needed new rawhide. I think he charged a dime, which seemed like a fair price.

Many other salesmen roamed the neighborhood, because most of the houses had mothers at home who needed items. The Fuller Brush man, the sweeper man, and the pots and pans man were other people I remember coming through the neighborhood during the 1950s.

Another worker went through the streets, driving a large horse-drawn cart and hollering the word "rags." Of course, we called him the "rag man." The ragman bought any sort of material, such as old clothing, sheets, and other things made of cloth. He also had a large scale behind his wagon where he weighed items. He paid a small amount of money to people for their excess clothing. The other kids and I liked the ragman because we enjoyed seeing a horse-driven carriage during those times. Also, we liked to look at his horse because it reminded us of the horses in the cowboy movies we loved to watch. The ragman came during the end of the era of horse-driven vehicles.

The scariest person visiting our neighborhood was the dogcatcher. He was an ominous man who would walk through the neighborhood looking for stray dogs. His name was Jack Young. Jack was a large older black man who wore an old police uniform, including a hat worn sideways on his head. Jack walked with a pronounced limp. Rumor had it he had been attacked by a dog, almost losing the use of his leg. Jack wore a holster with a large revolver around his waist. He usually had three or four leashed dogs following him that he had recently captured. Jack never smiled or spoke. No, he had a very intense look on his face as he walked and looked for stray dogs. We were all afraid of Jack Young. He probably was a nice guy, but we never stuck around long enough to find out. Stories about Jack Young were always shared among guys from different neighborhoods. They ranged from Jack battling wild dogs to him shooting dogs in the street. I don't know if any of those stories could be verified.

There were many other vendors that traveled through the neighborhood in the '50s. Milk trucks delivered fresh milk daily. I always liked to flag down a truck and buy a small bottle of fresh chocolate milk for seven cents if I had it. The Jewel Tea Company sent out trucks to sell various coffees, teas, and candies and cakes. Ladies gathered around the truck to buy items for their homes.

A couple other visitors came through our neighborhood only during the summer. I remember a photographer, who pulled a trailer with a pony in it. Kids then had their picture taken sitting on the pony and wearing a western outfit provided by the photographer. I really loved that pony.

18

1950 | Lou sitting on the pony—neighborhood
visitors included the photographer that brought a
pony to pose with the little guys and gals

Then there was the "ice ball man" (also known as the "snow cone guy"). He had a cart with a couple blocks of ice he scraped with a metal tool, gathering up smooth shaved ice to which he added flavored syrups and served delicious snow cones.

The ice ball man traveled the neighborhoods in the afternoon and ended up at a local baseball field. There he knew he could sell snow cones throughout the evening. We loved the ice ball man.

So many vendors and visitors passed through our neighborhood. It was busy during the day while the men were off to work. That has all changed now, and these vendors live on only in memory.

YO-YO MAN

OUR GROCERY STORE BROUGHT IN many different vendors. One of the most memorable of them arrived every spring. We knew him as the "Yo-Yo man," but he called himself the "Great Filipino."

I could not wait for the Yo-Yo man to bring his new supply of yo-yos each year. Mom, of course, was glad to sell them.

In case you have forgotten or never knew, a yo-yo is a small round wooden toy that fit in the palm of your hand. A string was wrapped around the middle of the yo-yo to allow the yo-yo to be thrown to the floor and return to your hand without hitting the floor.

You could perform loads of great tricks with a yo-yo. And the Great Filipino seemed to know them all. He scheduled a contest each year at various stores in the city.

The contests consisted of each boy or girl doing various tricks and competing against all the other contestants. The winner got a T-shirt and a fancy yo-yo. I won the contest one year. However, the Great Filipino decided to give the grand prize to the second-place runner-up the prize because my family owned the store. I did not mind since I ended up with a deluxe yo-yo and a T-shirt proclaiming me "Yo-Yo Champion."

I liked the "Great Filipino." He was a really nice guy and came to our store for five or six years during my younger days.

Yo-Yos, baseball cards, and kites were some of the neat stuff featured in our store during the spring months. So were paddles with a rubber ball connected onto a long rubber band. There were always things to keep us kids busy.

THE SHOEMAKER

OUR TOWN HAD A LOT of little shops where you could get your shoes repaired. Shoemakers could repair anything made of leather.

People who wore leather shoes maintained them by taking them to a fellow who owned a shoe repair business. There, he replaced soles and heels many times on a pair of shoes. Shoes were made so they could be disassembled and repaired like new.

When I got a new pair of shoes I knew it was supposed to last indefinitely or at least as long as they still fit me.

One of the favorite shoes for the young boys were known a "clodhoppers." They were high-top leather shoes with metal cleats on the heel and the toe. Guys liked clodhoppers because they could make a lot of noise when they walked on a hard surface. They lasted a long time, and I really liked mine.

During the summer, all of us young boys switched to high-top black tennis shoes. The top brand was Converse All-Stars, but I never got a pair of them when I was young. My folks picked out my tennis shoes at discount shoe stores because I was so hard on them.

Shoes were a big deal back then, and the shoemakers kept them in good shape. Sadly, we now live in a throwaway society. We don't seem to fix anything today.

PART 1:
Growing Up in the Fifties

DOWNTOWN AND ALL AROUND

DOWNTOWN

WE REFERRED TO THE BUSINESS district of our little city as "downtown." In truth, it amounted to five or six blocks of buildings along our main thoroughfare called Washington Street. Everything was located downtown. All the department stores, shoe stores, hardware stores, drugstores, jewelry shops, and bakeries were there.

Really, everything you might need was available in the downtown business district. Banks, our public library, and different government offices were also downtown. My favorite downtown stores were the five-and-dime stores, sporting goods stores, and soda shops.

All the parades were held downtown, with people marching down Washington Street. Sometimes thousands of people lined both sides of the street to watch the parade. Parades were held on all holidays, starting with Memorial Day at the end of May. Fourth of July, Halloween, and Armistice Day (now called Veterans Day) in November were other major dates when parades were organized.

In the 1950s, people loved a parade. The annual Christmas parade kicked off the holiday season in our town, a time that was so special there. Downtown stores always extended their evening hours to accommodate the increased shopping.

What I remember best is the wonderful Christmas displays stores placed in their windows facing the streets to show their wares. We loved to window-shop downtown at Christmastime. The hustle and bustle surpassed what went on there at any other time.

People were very friendly, and the crowded sidewalks gave you a good feeling on those cold holiday evenings. My parents, siblings, and I looked at all the department store windows. You should be able to guess which displays I liked the best. Yep, the ones that had all the new toys and the electric trains running.

All the movie theaters were located downtown. It was fun to see the upcoming advertisements at each theatre. The aroma of hot popcorn crept out into the area in front of the theater. It was enticing to say the least.

The nights we spent downtown before Christmas concluded with a hotdog or hamburger and a hot chocolate at one of the little diners located there.

I loved the downtown area during the 1950s, but I regret to say the stores are gone now. Fancy malls replaced those downtown stores, starting in the 1960s.

The automobile and working housewives were the main reasons the malls were developed. People needed more time to shop in the evenings and on weekends. The malls provided the parking and stores that led to the demise of the beautiful downtown areas of the 1950s.

BOWLING ALLEYS AND POOL HALLS

TWO OF OUR FAVORITE PLACES to head to as young guys in the 1950s were bowling alleys and pool halls. Not just to hang out either. Like a lot of my buddies, I worked at the bowling alleys setting pins. Keep in mind that back in the 1950s, alleys were not equipped with automatic pinsetters. They employed young guys to work behind each lane, retrieving the bowling ball and setting the bowling pins onto metal posts that ascended on the lane with a foot pedal operated by a different worker. Each pin had a hole drilled in the bottom so it could be placed correctly on the lane.

After setting the pins, the pinsetter had to jump onto the ledge surrounding the "pit." That was the name we gave to the area where the pins and ball landed on each roll. Sometimes a fellow setting pins would get hit with a flying pin, which made the job a little dangerous. That never bothered us.

No, the real reward came on Friday nights, after all the bowling leagues were finished. We were free to bowl until dawn on Saturday. It was a lot of fun working at the bowling alley during the 1950s.

Pool rooms, also known as "pool halls, were another place guys hung out during the 1950s. Not when we were very young; kids were not permitted in in pool halls.

Why not? Well, a lot of gambling took place in pool halls. People bet on just about everything that happened there, starting with the games of pool. At the same time, guys were playing cards for money. Men played poker all the time there. Although gambling was illegal, nobody enforced the laws when card games were going on at pool halls.

Sports betting also took place in pool halls. Many of them had a Western Union tickertape machine that constantly printed updated information on various sporting events. That noisy device monitored professional baseball, basketball, and football games. It also printed the results of horse races.

My folks never allowed me to go into the local pool halls when I was growing up. By the time I reached high school, though, I was a regular at those "dens of sin." Smart guy that I was, I never said anything about it at home.

Pool halls and everything that went on there seem pretty tame by today's standards. But they were a big part of city life in the 1950s.

NEWSSTANDS AND CONFECTIONARY STORES

MY BUDDIES AND I OFTEN went to the local newsstands and confectionary stores to buy baseball cards and comic books. Those spots were major parts of growing up in the '50s.

Boys loved reading comic books about super heroes. Superman and Batman topped the list. Too bad I did not save the dozens of comic books I accumulated throughout my youth. The newsstands always had the most recent copies of comic books, and we'd wait for them each month. Baseball cards were also bought there. I managed to keep most of the cards I collected during the 1950s, but flipping hurt their value.

The newsstands always had a unique smell. I remember it vividly and imagine it came from all the newspapers, magazines, candy, and tobacco they carried. Every newsstand smelled the same, and I really liked the smell. I would bet if many of were blindfolded and then put in a room with that smell, you would immediately know it was a newsstand.

Confectionary stores were not exactly like newsstands. They also stocked comic books, magazines, and baseball cards, but seldom sold various tobacco products. No, confectionary stores specialized in carrying endless kinds of candies. They sold boxes of chocolate for all the holidays. Some confectionary stores also had a soda fountain, where you could get an ice-cream cone or a milkshake.

These stores featured as well a wide selection of small toys and trinkets that were neat to look at. I bought a lot of my toy soldiers at a confectionary store near home.

You won't find many confectionary stores around today. One more casualty of "progress."

DINERS AND SODA SHOPS

SO MANY DINERS WERE AROUND in the 1950s. The first ones were built out of old railroad passenger cars remodeled into small restaurants. The typical diner consisted of a long counter with a row of swivel stools. There were also some booths around each side and tables by the front windows.

Every diner had a jukebox filled with great rock 'n' roll, rhythm & blues, and doo-wop songs. Each table and booth had a small chrome box on it against the wall connected to the main jukebox. You could flip through the songs posted on a metal carousel that contained the titles and numbers of all the songs in the jukebox. It cost a nickel to play one song, or you could get six songs for a quarter. Needless to say, the songs kept on coming from everyone in the diner.

Most of the diners operated 24 hours a day. There was always someone there. Kids would listen to the music, and sometimes they might even dance in the small area. We stopped in the evenings to get a hamburger and a genuine milkshake. My favorite was a fresh cheeseburger with grilled onions.

Soda shops were also favorite places to hang out in the 1950s. Most kids walked home from high school, and many had to walk through downtown to get home. Many of the drugstores had a soda fountain with some booths so people could have light dining and a good soda.

A lot of the kids stopped at the soda fountain on the way home from school to get an ice cream soda and chat with friends. The soda fountain also had a counter with swivel stools. The kids that worked behind the soda fountain were called "soda jerks." They made the very best milkshakes and ice cream sodas. You could also get a light sandwich or a hot dog at the drug store soda fountain

Many of the women who shopped in town during the day stopped at the soda fountain for a light lunch. But they cleared out before the kids descended upon the drug stores after school.

In the late 1950s, many kids, including me rushed home after school to flip on the TV to watch *American Bandstand*, hosted by Dick Clark. I had to watch if I knew he was going to feature a rock 'n' roll singer or group I liked.

American Bandstand stayed on the air for many more years. However, I think the peak came in the late 1950s and early '60s.

BARBERSHOPS

HAIRCUTS WERE 50 CENTS BACK in the day. If you wanted a close shave with a straight razor, you could get one for 25 cents. Yes, barbershops were humming back in the 1950s. Men and boys would get a haircut every two weeks. Hairstyles were short and neat. After all, all the guys liked to stay sharp.

Barbershops were all over the place. Most of them were downtown, but, many of them were scattered around the neighborhoods near some of the corner stores. Many of the barbers in our town were of Italian descent. That wasn't surprising because so many of the people there—about 40 percent—came from families that, like mine, had emigrated from Italy.

There was something about Italian men and cutting hair because when I was a little boy Dad always cut my hair at home. He did my cousins' hair, too. Well, maybe my father was not your typical guy. He owned all the barbering tools because he had studied to be a barber during his teenage years, when he had lived in Mahoningtown, Pennsylvania.

Dad told me he quit the barbering apprenticeship to take a job on the Pennsylvania Railroad. He quit because he could not stand the strong breath the old guys had who came in for a shave and a haircut. It sounded like a good reason to abandon that profession.

Dad continued to give all the family boys haircuts until they were 10 or 12 years old and started to go to modern barbershops for new-style haircuts. I'm talking about the teddy bear, the crew cut, and the flat top.

Of course, barbershops were more than just a place to get your hair cut back then. They were always filled with men who liked to socialize. Some barbershops in town had five or six barbers working at one time. There were also large sitting rooms, where men would talk sports and politics while they were waiting for a haircut.

I could not wait to get out of the barbershop, because getting my hair cut wasted a lot of time I could be out playing baseball or doing some other fun thing. My mother hollered at me if I did not get a haircut at least every two weeks.

We liked one barber who cut hair very fast. We called him Two-Minute Tony." Tony had a barbershop on a corner of a busy intersection with traffic light. It was said that Tony could start a haircut when the light was green and be finished before the light turned green again. I think that was an exaggeration, but Tony got you out of there fast.

When I got older, my cousin Frank, who came to America from Italy in the middle 1950s, started cutting my hair. Frank, who was about my age, went to school with me and then did his apprenticeship in barbering. He was my barber until he passed away a couple years ago.

Guys form a special relationship with their barber over the years. Somebody like Frank would see me at least every four weeks. He was "old-school" Italian and besides being my cousin was a good friend. I miss Frank.

Barbershops flourished during the 1950s but many of them started to close in the mid-1960s. Why? I will tell you in two words: The Beatles.

Longhair styles started to come into fashion, and boys and men stopped going to barbershops as often as they did before. Many barbers had to quit and find other professions.

The 50-cent haircuts were gone and so were many of the barbers. They were replaced by hair stylists, who cut your hair at 25 dollars a pop.

These simple times of the 1950s were gone, but not forgotten.

THE GAS STATION

THE AUTO INDUSTRY BOOMED IN the 1950s. As soldiers, sailors, and fliers returned from the war, many married, took jobs, and bought homes. And they wanted cars.

By the 1950s, many families were moving to suburbs, areas lying outside the main parts of cities. Automobiles were essential if you lived in the suburbs and wanted to work, shop, or visit downtown. With all the new cars came heightened demands for more service stations to sell the gasoline used in the automobiles.

In the past, gasoline was purchased at small stations that were called "filling stations." They generally had only one or two pumps next to a small building for the attendant. Quarts of motor oil were also sold there.

The 1950s changed all of that. Petroleum companies started to compete in the expanding market for gasoline needed to run the many thousands of cars being produced on assembly lines.

Companies such as Atlantic, Texaco, and Sunoco were building modern service stations all over the place. Commercials running on television encouraged drivers to use certain brands of gasoline.

I learned about gasoline in couple of ways when I was a youngster. First, there was the *Milton Berle Texaco Comedy Hour* on TV. Our family watched it every Tuesday evening. Second, sometime in the middle 1950s, Sunoco built a modern service station across from our corner grocery store on Taylor Street.

I was about 12 years old when the Sunoco station opened. The newly constructed facility included a large building that had two garage bays and an office. The new cement and pavement offset the beautiful blue-and-white siding on the new building. There were four islands outside, each having four individual gas pumps. The place was five times bigger than any filling station. The station had a large illuminated blue-red-yellow Sunoco arrow sign in the front. All the bright lights made the station really eye-catching during the night hours when it was open.

This made a great place for a 12-year-old boy to hang out and run errands for the service station workers. To show their thanks, the guys there gave me a blue cap with a Sunoco emblem on it. I really liked that hat and was the envy of all my buddies when I wore it. And I did every time I "worked" at the gas station. I learned a lot about cars at the Sunoco station and used the knowledge later when I was old enough to drive my own cars.

In the 1950s, oil companies could not do enough to encourage consumers to use their products. For example, all the attendants wore uniforms. Sunoco workers wore dark blue pants, a light blue shirt, and a blue hat. Their names and emblems were on the shirt and hat.

Whenever someone drove in to get gas, an attendant was waiting to pump it. He also offered to check the oil and tire pressure. And he always washed the front and rear windows.

Companies also gave trading stamps with every purchase. Customers saved the stamps to redeem for gifts at special centers. In the 1960s, among the gifts were electric train sets.

Boy, has everything changed! No more trading stamps or attendants at gas stations. Instead, you have to pump your own and pay for it inside the station if you don't rely on a credit card. You'll also be checking your own oil and tire pressure.

It is not uncommon to see a well-dressed woman in high heels putting gasoline into her new Mercedes-Benz at around $4.00 per gallon. That's a far cry from the 20 to 25 cents she would have paid in the 1950s. Go figure!

THE CUSTARD STAND

ONE OF THE FAVORITE PLACES we visited in the early 1950s was the local custard stand. By the way, don't confuse custard stand with General Custer's Last Stand.

Forbush Frozen Custard Stand opened in 1950 on Elwood Road. It was about six miles east of New Castle. And it is still in business as Forbush Drive-In, operated by descendants of the family that started it. No question to me that it was and still is the most delicious frozen custard of all time—firm yet still oh so smooth and creamy.

To set the record straight, frozen custard is not the same as ice cream. Custard is made with eggs, and ice cream is not. Also, ice cream is whipped and custard is slow turned to give it a dense and silky texture. There typically were only four flavors, all poured fresh from shiny metal machines.

During the summer months, Dad took us out for that delicious treat. There were always long lines at Forbush's, but it was worth the wait. You could get a hand-dipped ice-cream cone anywhere in the 1950s. Same with an ice-cream cone at all the eating places and the drug stores with a soda fountain.

One of the best places to buy an ice-cream cone was at the Isaly stores (a chain of family-owned dairies and restaurants in the Midwest). They featured the "Skyscraper," an ice-cream cone made with a long scoop and placed on a cone. Isaly's ice cream was very tasty, and they had many flavors. Two of my favorites were called rainbow and white house cherry. Isaly's also had a nice soda bar, where you could buy any kind of milkshake, sundae, or ice cream soda.

In the mid-1950s, the first Dairy Queen opened on the south side of our town. The beauty of that Dairy Queen was it being in walking distance of my home and on my way to school. The day of the grand opening, the Dairy Queen gave out free sundaes all day. My buddies and I spent the entire day in line there. I think I had twelve different sundaes that day.

I liked the frozen custard at Dairy Queen, but it could never compare to the custard at Forbush's. By the way, even though that Dairy Queen is no longer there, there are two other ones in our town.

That reminds me of the line from the great comedian Red Buttons: "Show me a milkman in high heels, and I'll show you a dairy queen!"

DRIVE-INS

WITH THE INCREASE OF AUTOMOBILES in the 1950s, a new type of eating service emerged. Small roadside restaurants started serving people while they sat in their cars parked in front. Customers pulled up and beeped the horn to notify the waitress, or carhop as we called them, they wanted to place an order. She went out to the car and took the food order.

Once the order had been filled, the carhop returned to the auto with a tray and hung a tray-holder on the driver's side window elevated enough to hook the holder. Usually, these drive-in restaurants served burgers and sandwiches, as well as soft drinks and milkshakes.

When customers finished their meal, they blinked the headlights to tell the carhop to return with the bill and collect the tray. The carhops usually received a nice tip for the service.

Soon, drive-in restaurants popped up all over. In our town, a Big Boy drive-in restaurant was constructed in the mid-1950s. It was part of a chain, so Big Boy restaurants were in many towns. They were more modern than the older roadside drive-ins.

The Big Boy restaurants had large parking lots. The stands where cars parked featured a lighted menu and electronic speakers for placing the food order.

Meanwhile, carhops were becoming more up to date, right down to wearing caps and short skirts. Some places had carhops serving meals on roller skates. Too bad our town missed out on that change!

The drive-in restaurant became a great place for teenagers and young adults to hang out in the 1950s. Car cruises originated there, as guys parking their cars and ate all night long.

The drive-in craze slowed down in the late 1950s, when McDonald's opened its fast food restaurants. People demanded quick, cheap service when they drove into a McDonald's. They ate the food fast and never left a tip.

I miss drive-in restaurants and being able to pull in and eat a well-cooked meal in the comfort of my car. Everyone seems to be in a hurry to eat that fast food junk.

Along with drive-in restaurants came the introduction of drive-in movies. They were outdoor theaters with large parking lots that had spaces equipped with a pole and an electric speaker. The speaker was attached to the driver's side window, and people watched a movie projected on a very large screen in the front of the parking lot.

The outdoor theatres let people, mostly families and couples, enjoy a movie in their car. Drive-ins operated mostly in the spring and the summer and closed during the winter months. Some drive-ins tried giving electric heaters to customers when they opened during the cold months.

Drive-ins were, as many of you remember very well, popular dating venues for young adults. I loved the dollar-a-carload special nights when our local drive-in ran B-rated movies. We stuffed eight or nine guys in the car, including a couple in the trunk.

Too bad most of the drive-ins are gone, but they were great attractions back in the day.

SWIMMING HOLES

YOUNG GUYS LIKED TO GO swimming on those hot summer days in the 1950s. Luckily for us, there were a few places to swim in our town. Two rivers ran through New Castle. The Shenango River was on the west side of the city, and Neshannock Creek was on the east side. Both of them came to a point on the south side, where they combined to form the Mahoning River, which flowed south of the county.

When I was a boy, the Shenango River was big, deep, and dirty. Waste from many of the steel mills north of town flowed into it. We never swam in that river.

Neshannock Creek had and still does have two personalities. It usually was a clean and shallow body of fresh water. But a rainstorm could turn it into a raging waterway capable of causing a lot of flood damage.

Back in the 1950s, people made dams all along the creek to create swimming holes. That was where we generally went swimming when I was a boy.

A bridge crossed Neshannock Creek at Washington Street. We called it the "penny bridge" because there was a swimming hole below the bridge where boys swam. People threw coins into the water, and boys would dive for them. The most popular time was during lunch hours on business days. It was fun to dive for the coins. Better yet, it was profitable.

Proceeding up Neshannock Creek were many other swimming holes. Most of them were made by natural rock formations and other structures. Some of the names of the swimming holes were: Horse Fly, Paper Mill Bridge, Flat Rock, and the Cinders.

Farther up Neshannock Creek was a small privately owned picnic area known as El Rio Beach. A small section of the water had been dammed to create a nice swimming area. There was no sand on this beach. Small pebbles were put there to serve as a beach.

At El Rio Beach you would find a bathhouse, and a few picnic shelters with tables. There were also a ball field and a dance hall.

Since you had to pay to use El Rio Beach, we didn't go there very often. We preferred to swim down the creek for free. El Rio Beach has been gone for many years now.

We swam in the swimming holes during my younger years. Once I reached my teenage years, my friends and I migrated to Cascade Park and other public pools. One big reason for the change: The pools were where we'd find the girls!

CASCADE PARK

IN THE 1950S, THERE WERE many small amusement parks in towns across America. Those parks were not nearly the size of the mega amusement parks of today. My family and I were lucky to have in our town a small amusement park called Cascade Park. It was located on two hills divided by a valley with a stream known as Big Run Creek running through it. The fact that Big Run Creek had waterfalls that formed pools of water led to the name of Cascade Park. The local news company had launched a contest to name the new park being developed at the turn of the 20th century. The person who won the contest suggested Cascade Park because of the water that would cascade over the waterfalls on Big Run Creek.

The land where Cascade Park (or "the park," as everyone called it) was developed was a beautiful wooded area. The owner of the scenic land gave it to our city with the stipulation that it would remain a park as long as the city owned it. In its early years, Cascade Park served as a picnic area. Ongoing improvements made possible additional recreational activities. For example, constructing a dam at the lower end of the park formed a lake for swimming and boating.

By the 1950s, Cascade Park had become a delightful amusement park. Rides included a roller coaster erected on the natural hilly terrain called "the gorge." The wooden roller coaster was the main attraction among the fourteen or so adult rides that were there in the 1950s. There was also a nice kiddie land. A penny arcade included many neat games. Ski-Ball alleys were always a favorite of our gang. We liked to play each other and collect tickets based on high scores tallied on each game. We saved the tickets that were cashed in for prizes at the end of summer.

One of my favorite rides was the miniature train ride. It was a replica of a B&O diesel passenger train. It consisted of two miniature diesel engines and five or six coaches that would seat adults and children in the open air. The train would start at the station and circle around to the main line. It would then cross the in park road that was equipped with really nice miniature flashing railroad crossing signals, complete with ringing bells.

The train would then cross a bridge over the Big Run stream. It then proceeded to the other side of the park under a tunnel to the swimming pool area. The train would then circle the pool area and head back to the station. I loved to ride the train and look at all of the beautiful natural scenery of the park. Every time we walked to the park to go swimming we would always take a ride on the train before we headed home.

Food concession stands could be found around the park and the midway. I will never forget the great French fries known as "Park Fries." The amusement rides were set up on one of the two hilly sections of the park. The lower section included a picnic grove with six or seven covered pavilions that had many picnic tables. The lake also on the lower area provided boat rides and fishing. On the other side of the two hills were three magnificent swimming pools: a large wading pool, a long rectangular shallow pool, and a large circular deep pool with one high and two low diving boards. The swimming area could accommodate many people and was always kept in pristine condition.

There was a large two-story bathhouse. Its top floor was open on one side and housed a large grandstand. In the 1950s, people (mostly parents and grandparents) sat in the grandstands to watch the bathers. Spectators sat in the grandstands to view various swimming events. We spent many days at the pool during the summer months. Local organizations and other groups held picnics at the grove while everyone enjoyed the park. The park seemed to have some sort of day for every organization in town.

In addition, Cascade Park had a huge dance pavilion. Visiting groups enjoyed using the pavilion. I remember it being the site of sock-hops during my high school years.

These parks are all gone today. But back in the '50s, Cascade Park was the major place used by everyone in the town and surrounding communities. The small amusement parks are a missed part of today's slice of Americana.

PART 1:
Growing Up in the Fifties

FUN WITH MY FRIENDS

CATHOLIC SCHOOL

MY FAMILY BELONGED TO A Roman Catholic church with the name St. Vitus. Besides going with my parents to mass, I attended the school there. The first school at St. Vitus parish opened in 1952. It consisted of kindergarten through third grade. The building was large enough to house nine grades. For that reason, the church added an additional grade every year until it reached the maximum of nine grades.

One thing that I did not like was that Catholic School loaded the students with a lot of homework. My friends that attended Public school never had the homework that we had.

We liked the Holy days that we were give off during the school year (there were eight). We did not like the extra days that we had to make up in June when everyone else was on summer vacation.

Nuns of the Sacred Heart Order taught school. The sisters of the Sacred Heart were highly educated. Most of them had masters and doctoral degrees. They taught during the school year and attended graduate school in the summer.

I started St. Vitus school in the initial second grade class. I continued to go there until I finished ninth grade. The nuns were excellent teachers but for the most part were very strict. They were purveyors of guilt, which I think they learned from my mother. They were quick to remind us of the punishment we would get for any unwarranted behavior both here and in the afterlife.

We started each day during the school year by attending morning mass at our church. It stood next to the school. The church was where we celebrated every holiday with the appropriate High Mass. We learned to sing at mass in Latin, English, and sometimes in Italian. I liked to sing in church. One sister said we had "the voices of angels." We sung our heads off.

Each day at school opened with our first-period class on religion. There, we learned about our faith. Many times a priest taught the class instead of a nun. I liked learning about my religion. However, I would agree with many of my buddies, who thought over the nine years we were "over-churched."

1952 | First second grade class of St. Vitus School
Lou is second boy on left in the second row

At our school, boys were required to wear white shirts, ties and dress pants (no blue jeans). The girls had matching skirts and blouses. I hated the dress code, but eventually got used to it.

The nuns were dressed head to toe in black, except for the white stiff linen piece of material that covered their forehead. Only their face and hands were unclothed. When I first saw the nuns I thought they had wheels under them as they motored around in the long floor-length black skirt.

The nuns usually kept their arms under their black blouse. They took them out only at certain moments. Arms would appear magically, only to write something on the chalkboard or hit kids who were misbehaving.

Yes, the stereotype of nuns using use a wooden ruler to administer punishment to the kids by slapping them on their hands with it had plenty of truth behind it. I wonder how that would go over today.

Of course, I never told Mom or Dad about receiving such a punishment. If I had, they would have administered the same at home—and possibly harder!

The sisters were intelligent and taught school in an excellent manner. They bestowed on all of us the values of life. They had many great stories related to their teachings that helped us learn.

I had many buddies during my years at St. Vitus in the 1950s. They treated me as their unofficial leader. We got into mischief which was all in good fun and made our years at school more tolerable.

There was a unique brotherhood formed among all the kids that went to school with me. I would not trade that education for any other.

Looking back, I could write a book dedicated to the Catholic school experience of the 1950s. Maybe I will someday.

1957 | Lou's 7th grade gang acting crazy in the school yard at St. Vitus

SNOWBALL FIGHTS

A FEW DAYS AFTER CHRISTMAS, we'd start to collect the dried Christmas trees being discarded in the backyards of every house in our neighborhood. No artificial trees back then; everyone had a live Christmas tree.

People knew kids collected the discarded trees. But no one—at least not the adults—had a clue about what we did with them.

So I'll let you in on the secret. We kids dragged the trees to our baseball field, which was not used during the winter months. We divided the trees and made three or four forts arranged in a circle. We ended up with small cabins where we built campfires to keep us warm.

When we got older, say around 12 or 13, we found another use for those cabins. They gave us the ideal spot to smoke cigarettes. Our parents weren't around to scold us or take them away.

Once snow fell, the snowball fights would begin. We'd pile up a bunch of snowballs as ammunition in the wars between the cabins.

The snowball fights would last all day or until someone got smacked in the eye. Then we called a truce to make sure he wasn't blind. To my knowledge, no one was ever seriously hurt during our snowball fights. Once the snowballs were gone, we grabbed our sleds and went riding.

CARNIVALS

OUR NEIGHBORHOOD WAS NEXT TO a large field that had among other features two baseball diamonds. The city cleared out another large area donated for recreational activities. It was called Dean Park, probably after the person who donated the property. City officials decided to have a carnival on one of the large fields to make money for further development of the ballparks.

Our gang loved the week when the carnival was set up in the field. Starting the day the trucks first rolled in, we headed over to get jobs from the carnival people. They needed water and other items we bought and delivered to their tents and trailers. They paid us with a little money and a lot of ride tickets.

"Carnies," as the people working at the carnival were known, seemed to me to be very interesting. They appeared happy and worked hard. They had to move from town to town, entertaining people. To a young boy, everything about carnies seemed neat.

The rides were set up, and food trailers and games occupied the midway. The carnivals also had sideshows featuring some pretty weird acts. It was interesting to see these acts during the day as they walked around before the shows started. I got an unforgettable firsthand look at carnival people and carnival life.

Everything came to a climax on Saturday night. There was a fireworks display, and a man was shot out of a cannon into a net. Then the entire carnival was packed up and rolled out the next day, on its way to another city.

It took us weeks to clean the grounds after the carnival left so we could play baseball on the field. But the week the carnival was there made all the mess worthwhile!

THE CIRCUS

WHEN THE CIRCUS CAME TO town, the workers set up everything first in another part of the city.

The circus arrived by train and unloaded at the local station. Soon there was a long line of wagons pulled by horses and small tractors.

The parade of vehicles marched through the business district to the part of town where they were going to set up. There was a marching band. People lined the streets to watch the circus parade.

My friends and I naturally followed the parade. Then we stayed out there all day, watching the setup and asking for jobs.

My favorite part of the circus was the food tent. I loved the smell of fried onions cooking on the grill, along with the hot dogs and hamburgers. I never ate a better hamburger than those served at the circus food tent.

Sometimes the Ringling Bros. and Barnum & Bailey show came to our town. More often, we saw the Cole Bros. Circus. They were all great.

The wild animals on display and performing thrilled me. The elephants were some of my favorites. They were huge and well trained. I loved watching all the elephants parade, marching in order around the main ring.

STREET BASKETBALL

BEFORE WE HAD BASKETBALL COURTS built by the city at local playgrounds, we played street basketball. The game was simple and straightforward.

First, we picked a telephone pole on a paved street in our neighborhood to be our basketball court. The pole should have a light on it so we were able to play at night. Usually, the traffic was much less in the evenings on a dead-end street.

Next, we made a backboard out of wood. Then we had to attach a rim we had purchased.

Climbing a stepladder, the bigger guys hoisted up the board, so it was 10 feet from the ground. Then we had to nail it to the wooden telephone pole. Finally, we attached a couple of 2 by 4 wooden braces from the side of the backboard to the goal.

Once we had put up our basket, we were ready to play. We spent countless hours playing street basketball throughout the fall to the spring.

We chose teams and played tournaments. Every kid got a chance to play, although some of the smaller guys did not get many shots.

Today, I doubt that kids would even look at our small street basketball court. That's okay. We had to make a lot out of a little.

ROCK 'N' ROLL MUSIC

I WAS IN SEVENTH GRADE in 1956, when my oldest sister gave me my first record player. It was an RCA 45-rpm phonograph. Made of durable plastic, it could play seven or eight disks stacked on a spindle that had a large red top. The record player was able to play one song over and over or automatically play the records stacked on the large spindle.

That gift started me listening to and collecting records. Specifically, records booming the new genre of music dubbed rock 'n' roll.

The new records I loved were priced at 45 cents each, which was a lot of money for 12-year-old.

Still, I manage to purchase a couple records. Once I had them home, I played them constantly in my bedroom. My buddies came over, bringing some of their disks. We spent the night absorbing the new music.

Danny & the Juniors had a huge hit in early 1958 called, *At the Hop*. They were the first rock group I liked. I bought a transistor radio and listened to the Pittsburgh channels during the day. We somehow picked up stations in New York City and Chicago stations at night.

We knew all the songs and memorized all the lyrics of those early rock 'n' roll songs. From then on, our boyhood hobbies and activities took second place to listening to music. Even our toy trains didn't seem as special and important anymore.

GARAGE BANDS

ONCE MY BUDDIES AND I started to listen to rock 'n' roll, we decided we'd like to play the music. Fortunately for us, most kids learned to play some kind of musical instrument during those days.

The guys and I gathered together and played songs we were able to learn. There was no place in anybody's home where we could practice without causing a ruckus. And the houses weren't big enough to accommodate a group of teenagers blowing horns and singing at the top of their lungs.

Our solution then, as kids in rock bands have discovered ever since, was the garage. We found several of them where we could play rock 'n' roll to our hearts' content.

The garage bands were a lot of fun. In the later years, we had better instruments and amplifiers and so could make better and more polished sounds. That ushered us into the middle 1960, what we called the Beatle Years.

But the four-part harmony popular years before remains my favorite genre of rock. What people refer to as doo-wop music. We sang lots of that in dusty garages and always sounded smooth.

TRANSISTOR SISTER

IN 1950, OUR FAMILY HAD a portable radio made by what was then known as the Zenith Radio Corporation. Back in the day, portable radios were large and heavy—and not very reliable.

Our Zenith radio was the size of a small carry-on suitcase with a handle. It used vacuum tubes and a large square battery that did not last too long and cost a lot to replace. All we could get on our Zenith were AM stations. We didn't mind because there weren't many FM stations then. Most of the time our portable radio sat on the kitchen counter. Mom kept it plugged into a wall socket rather than waste the expensive battery.

Sometime in the middle 1950s, some American companies began introducing transistor radios. A revolution was in the making. A tiny transistor replaced the glass tubes used in the older radios. Small batteries powered the new transistor radios.

Naturally, our family had to have one of the new gadgets. So Mom bought a transistor radio made in America by our family our first Transistor radio by the Emerson Radio Corporation. The new radio was a lot smaller than the bulky Zenith portable radio. It was the size of a cigar box.

I loved that transistor radio from the start. Best thing about it was the earphone, which made it possible for me to listen to ball games and rock music in bed without bothering anybody trying to sleep.

My parents paid about $45 for our transistor radio. That was a lot of money in the 1950s: about $425 dollars at today's prices. But it was worth it, especially to my mother, who enjoyed listening to the radio on the porch in the summer.

The Japanese got into the act later in the 1950s. They managed to produce smaller transistor radios that cost less than half of what American companies had charged.

Japan started to flex its technology muscles, and the American people bought their products. Why not? Their radios were smaller, better, and cheaper, even if they competed successfully against American technology.

The transistor radios kept coming, and the American teenagers were buying them like crazy. All of us loved listening to rock music on our little radios. They fueled record sales and planted the seeds for the new radio stations arriving on the scene.

In 1961, the popular rock singer Freddy "Boom-Boom" Cannon recorded a song titled, "Transistor Sister." It described how teenagers were playing their transistor radios.

Today, transistor radios are not the items of choice for listening to music. Kids have all the latest electronics used to listen to music and do many other things on an instrument smaller and thinner than a pack of cigarettes.

iPhones and iPods can store thousands of songs that can be recalled in an instant. I still have a flip-phone, and it does not play music. I also have a transistor radio that I use around the house. But that's me.

THE GREAT FIRES

WHEN WINTER CAME TO AN end, the kids in our neighborhood, including me, started planning our annual great fire.

The Christmas tree forts we had built on the baseball field had to be removed. What better way to get rid of the large piles of dried-up pine and fir trees than to have a large bonfire? We stacked hundreds of trees into a huge pile. As I recall, the pile could be higher than 30 feet!

We waited for a calm evening in early March and gathered the gang together to light this great fire. The flames shot hundreds of feet into the night sky. The fire burned quickly yet gave a magnificent light. It was an incredible sight.

The neighbors who lived near the field understood what we were doing every year. Did they mind a little arson? No way! They were thankful we got rid of their trees every Christmas season. We stood by the fire the entire evening as it smoldered. Once the blaze was out, we had a new frame of mind.

You see, the annual fire represented the end of winter and the official start of spring. And spring meant one thing—baseball.

So we kids spent the next two or three weeks cleaning and refurbishing the baseball field to get it ready for the new season.

SLED RIDING

WE HAD A COUPLE ALLEYS in our neighborhood that were on small hills. And they were perfect for riding sleds during the snowy winter.

Black Top Hill was our favorite place to ride. It was a paved alley that had very little traffic. After the snow was deep enough, we would prepare that alley for sled riding. We all had sleds, and everybody turned out when it snowed.

Black Top Hill had a streetlight, which made it possible for us to sled ride in the evening. The slope was fast and short, and a rider had to be careful not to go too far into the high traffic street that crossed the end of the alley.

No cars would travel through the alley once we had prepared it for sled riding. Even the city workers who salted the various streets knew there was no need to salt our alley and ruin the sled riding.

THE ORANGE CRATE DERBY

ON LABOR DAY EVERY YEAR during the 1950s the local Optimus Club would sponsor The Orange Crate Derby. The event challenged kids in our county to build a non-motorized cart to race against other contestants.

Our city called it the Orange Crate Derby. Elsewhere, similar events were called Soap Box Derbies. In the early days, kids built their carts from wood they scavenged from old orange crates and boxes for soap. You can figure out how the races got their names.

The carts had to constructed along specific guidelines. However, when Derby Day came you knew kids did not make the beautiful racecars they brought. Plenty of parental help was indicated.

The event was held on Taylor Street. That road was in our neighborhood, but none of us ever managed to build a professional type of derby racecar. Fortunately, we were able to watch the Orange Crate Derby every year, along with the thousands of people that lined both sides of Taylor Street (blocked off for that day).

My parents owned a grocery store on the corner of Pearson and Taylor Streets, so they set up a nice concession stand for that day. They sold ice cream, soda pop, potato chips, candy, and balloons that day. I really liked Labor Day and the Orange Crate Derby.

The event ended in 1961, I think liability insurance put the kibosh to the race. Of course, we didn't need an organized race to give us a reason to build our own makeshift go-carts. Our carts might have been primitive, but we made them ourselves without parental help. We got wheels from anywhere we could. Old baby buggies, wagons, and anything else that rolled were great sources. We attached the wheels to 2 x 4 pieces of wood. Then we put them on the wood that made the axles for the carts.

Old doors made good frames for the homemade go-carts. We steered the carts with pieces of rope strapped to the 2 x 4 axles we had bolted to the wooden frame.

We raced the carts on the same hill that in the winter was our favorite for sled riding. We had to move around to different hills because the road traffic made it impossible for us to race the carts on various streets.

We did not race our go-carts very often, but it was fun when we did.

PART 1:
Growing Up in the Fifties

GROWING UP AND GETTING OLDER

BICYCLES

MOST FAMILIES OWNED ONLY ONE car in the 1950s. To be honest, many had none. If the kids wanted to go anywhere, they had to walk. Parents did not cart around their children to visit friends or go to the movies or anywhere else.

For kids, the main mode of transportation was a bicycle. I had learned to ride a two-wheel bicycle by the time I finished first grade. It was a big deal to be able to balance on a two-wheel bicycle. It was a rite of passage, and your peers no longer considered you a little kid. Instead, you could ride with all the bigger kids in the neighborhood.

Once I had conquered that feat, my parents bought me a J.C. Higgins 20-inch two-wheeler. Then I was ready to join all the other kids. We went everywhere on our bikes, usually riding in groups of youngsters about our own age. We would ride downtown to the movies. There were always bike stands, where we could park a bunch of bicycles while we attended the movies. Nobody seemed to bother the bicycles in those days. I wouldn't try that now unless I had a good lock and chain. Today, people would probably steal the bicycle *and* the stand.

1951 | Lou's first J.C. Higgins 20" bike. Dad's 1948 Buick Roadmaster Torpedo back in background

We loved our bicycles and were able to maintain them. If we needed parts, we headed to any of the many shops that sold new and used bicycles as well as parts. They also did the repairs we couldn't figure out.

I rode my first bicycle for a few years until I grew out of it. My parents later bought me a used Schwinn 26-inch English racer from an older boy in our neighborhood. The three-speed English racer had the traditional skinny tires and was very fast. It also climbed hills easily. It was fun to ride. We traveled all around the area with our bicycles. Sometimes we rode out of town and camped overnight in the countryside.

1957 | Lou with his Schwinn English Racer

My English racer was a vast improvement over the heavy bicycles with fat tires and no gears. When we went on the long trips, I felt sorry for the guys that did not have a racer.

Kids today do not seem to ride bikes as we did back in the day. Everything has changed. Most of the kids get chauffeured everywhere they want to go, and so they're missing the fun we had going places on our bicycles. It made us feel good and learn to be independent.

TOYS

GROWING UP IN THE 1950s, we played with many toys of all different types. Kids liked to emulate actors starring on TV programs and in the movies. Hopalong Cassidy, Roy Rogers, Gene Autry, and the Lone Ranger were my favorite cowboys when I grew up.

Boys loved playing cowboys and Indians, so they looked up to the heroes of westerns. They begged their parents for six-shooter cap pistols with holsters. All of us owned toy holsters, and rifles we used to reenact scenes in the movies we had recently watched.

Boys also had play army helmets and toy guns we used to replay World War II movies playing at that time. Our favorite army hero was John Wayne.

Another way we recreated the movies and TV programs we watched was to play with miniature metal soldiers, cowboys, and Indians. I spent hours during the winter playing with my toy soldiers and cowboys. I recall setting them up in the corner of our living room, where I played with them while watching westerns on our black-and-white TV.

In the summer, my friends and I moved the soldiers and cowboys to our front porch. There, we arranged them on the nice carpet.

Today, unfortunately, I don't think kids play that way. Instead, they spend a lot of time playing video games and monkeying around with their smart phones.

That's really too bad. I think we had more fun with our miniature figures in the 1950s.

Girls in the 1950s played with dolls, in preparation for being moms when they grew up. A lot of girls also had neat metal two-story dollhouses. The dollhouses were modern six-room homes large enough to hold different little figures and furniture. The dollhouses were open in the back. That made it easy for kids to set up the furniture and arrange the dolls.

Boys had similar metal buildings to enjoy. But they were designed and decorated to look like the storefront of a town in the Old West. I remember one kind of one-piece structure that had a sheriff's office, a saloon, and a couple other typical businesses. The back was open so you could reach and move around cowboy figures and various details. My western town came from Louis Marx & Company. It was called a Roy Rogers western play set, and I spent lots of time with it.

Of course, my all-time favorite toy when I was a kid was my electric train set. Almost every kid had one back then, and you felt sorry for the ones who did not. Families set up their Lionel, American Flyer, or Marx train at Christmas every year. Those were the top lines of trains during the 1950s, which I consider the Golden Age of Toy Trains.

I have written dozens of stories about collecting and running toy trains, and you'll find many of them in my first book: *I Never Met a Train I Didn't Like.*

Thinking about that title, I guess you could refer to the second part of this book as *I Still Haven't Met a Train I Didn't Like.*

Another favorite activity for kids in the 1950s was playing board games. A favorite of mine came from the Tudor Company. It developed an electric football game with figures vibrating on a scale metal field. Monopoly was another game popular with kids of all ages.

There were so many other toys kids across America played with in the 1950s. Two-wheel scooters, Radio Flyer wagons, metal street roller skates, doll buggies, Robbie the Robot, Erector Sets from A.C. Gilbert, Lincoln Logs, and Tinker Toys were a few classics I remember.

But I can't finish this general description of toys from the 1950s without mentioning two newer ones that now are in the National Toy Hall of Fame. Wham-o introduced the Hula Hoop in 1958, and it became a national rage. Every kid wanted one! A year later, Mattel brought out the first of its Barbie dolls. Girls loved them and still play with them.

PAPER ROUTE

I GOT MY FIRST JOB as a Sunday paperboy. Earning that way made it possible for me to buy some of the records I wanted while also having extra spending cash. I got a paper route in our neighborhood to deliver Sunday papers. Each Sunday, after attending 7 o'clock mass with my parents, I deliver my Sunday papers. Mom fixed breakfast for me, and I prepared the papers for delivery. The bundles of papers were delivered to our corner store. Dad and I assembled the Sunday papers, stuffing the news sections with all the advertisements.

I had more than 200 customers, so once the papers were ready, I stacked them in a wooden wagon with high sides to keep the papers from falling out and blowing away. The newspaper company provided the wagon to me at no charge. I pulled the wagon throughout the entire neighborhood, hand-delivering a paper to each customer. I started at 8 o'clock and was usually finished by 1 in the afternoon.

Of course, I wanted to be done sooner so I could spend more time having fun with my friends. So I employed some of them to help deliver the papers, paying them with candy and soda pop I bought after delivering everything. No one objected. We all realized the sooner I got done, the quicker we could start our Sunday afternoon activities: movies, baseball, football, or whatever else we did during each season.

It was good to have a paper route, even though it required a commitment. That was my first experience in business. I learned that without a commitment to the job, no matter what the job was, it couldn't be successful.

I liked the Christmas season because customers appreciated my service and tipped me at least $1.00. Keep in mind that was big money to a kid back in the day.

POLIO

NOT ALL OF MY EARLY memories were happy ones. Like every other kid in the early 1950s, I was aware of the fear during the summer months of the deadly disease, polio.

Youngsters everywhere were constantly being warned about contracting polio. We were told it could spread very easily among young children. I remember we were afraid to go to the public swimming pools. Everyone thought the disease was spread easier in those environments.

The sight of children in wheelchairs and braces was all too common during the early 1950s. We heard about the iron lungs kids stricken with polio were put in to help them breathe.

The nation breathed a collective sigh of relief when Dr. Jonas Salk of Pittsburgh, Pennsylvania, discovered a vaccine that could prevent this dreaded disease.

Every boy and girl were vaccinated against polio before entering school. The vaccination left a small scar in the upper arm. It served as a reminder of the victory over this terrible disease.

TELEVISION

SO MUCH CHANGED MY GENERATION from those that came before. But nothing had a bigger impact than television. We were the first group to be raised with a television in the home.

I can remember my aunt being the first on our street to have a TV set. Her family purchased a small black-and-white TV in early 1951. My family and I visited them on special evenings when something was on that we wanted to watch, anything from Milton Berle to *Studio One* to professional wrestling. All of us gathered in their living room to enjoy this new invention called TV.

A few months later, my family got its first TV—a Crosley 16-inch black-and-white console. I was in second grade when we bought our first TV.

Other kids came over to my house to watch anything on TV. *Howdy Doody* was one of our early favorites. Month by month more programs were added, and the TV generation was born. Eventually, every family had a TV in its home. Playtime ended up diminished, at least at first.

People were glued to their television sets and would watch anything broadcast on that small black-and-white tube in their living rooms. Families gathering around a TV replaced evening conversations at the dinner table. In many homes, parents and kids ate off small metal folding tables called "TV dinner trays."

Not in the Palumbo household! My mother never put up with that form of dining behavior. She insisted on the continuation of eating the dinner meal in our kitchen. Sometimes I had to force my supper down so I would not miss much of the early evening westerns on TV.

In the beginning, there were few TV stations over which we could receive a good picture.

Aluminum television antennas cropped up on every home that got their first TV. In our area, we could receive only signals from channels in Pittsburgh. The reception was not always clear, and many times the program was watched with a less-than-perfect picture. The term "snowy picture" was common on many of the viewing evenings.

Of course, TV was a new phenomenon back in the early 1950s. It did not make up the majority of entertainment hours.

However, the number of stations grew, as did the number of programs on each station. By the late 1950s, we were receiving ten to fifteen channels from Youngstown, Ohio, and Pittsburgh.

Television rapidly became the main form of information and entertainment, replacing newspapers, radio, and motion pictures. During the late 1950s color TV also was viewed in many homes.

A lot was gained with the invention of the television. But as Mom seemed to know, the family union suffered under this phenomenon in ways that would consume the nation in years to come.

THE MOVIES

TELEVISION HAD LIMITED PROGRAMS in the 1950s. After all, there were only a few stations broadcasting in our town. We kids turned for entertainment to the local movie theaters. Luckily, we could walk to the theaters located downtown. All our neighborhoods were close to the center of tow.

During the week, old western, comedy, and science fiction movies were shown at 4 o'clock. We managed to see a movie once or twice a week. I remember getting to the theater at that time for a double feature (not something kids today can imagine). We paid 9 cents to watch cartoons, a newsreel, coming attractions, and two movies and still be back home by 8 o'clock. Another penny got me a couple of Walnettos to munch.

These movies were shown early so the regular feature could start after the ushers had cleared out the theater. That was fine with us because we had to go home anyways. On Friday night, theaters played the scary movies. The original *Frankenstein* and *The Wolf Man* were two of my favorites. I never knew life could be so good.

Movie theaters were major parts of life for any child growing up in the 1950s. We got a real (or reel, to use a bad pun) education from the movies and the newsreels shown there.

Parents never had to worry about the content of the movies. The language was always G-rated, even though those categories didn't exist back then. Violence was limited to westerns, Army movies, and what occurred during the scary horror films was nothing compared to what you can see today.

The memories were so good that I still watch those old movies today over different cable channels. My favorites continue to be westerns and war films. They bring me "back in the day."

During the holiday season, theatres had special Saturday morning programs. They showed 21 color cartoons, followed by a first-run western or comedy feature.

Movie theaters also sold chances for 5 cents each or 6 for a quarter during the four weeks prior to Christmas. Then came the Saturday before Christmas. We arrived at 9 o'clock and couldn't wait until they announced the winning ticket holder. That lucky kid was awarded a beautiful new bicycle. No, I never won a bike, but did take home some of the smaller gifts raffled off. Everyone there received a free bag of candy. We were home by 1 o'clock.

After the movies we'd visit all the stores that had Christmas train displays running. The perfect ending to the perfect day back then. Yes, those days were choice and never to be duplicated.

COMMUNISTS

DURING THE EARLY 1950s, ONE of the biggest fears we had was being infiltrated and taken over by Communists.

The Soviet Union was considered a major threat to the United States after World War II. People worried about them sending spies and subversive groups to America to undermine our government. Everyone, even the grown-ups, seemed afraid Communists were secretly infiltrating for an eventual takeover.

We were raised with that fear of Communists. So we always had to be aware of them, especially since we didn't know who they were. Hollywood capitalized on this pervasive fear with movies and even a TV series called, *I Led Three Lives*. The programs focused on a man who was a dual agent with the FBI and the Communist party.

I'll be honest with you: *I Led Three Lives* scared the crap out of me. Each show presented situations related to everyday life, so you were left imagining there was a Commie behind every corner.

Time—and a lack of a true takeover by Russia—cured most of these fears. But as most of us remember, back in the day they felt much too real.

BOMB SHELTERS

THE FEAR OF A TAKEOVER by the Soviet Union never seemed worse or more intense than when we had air raid practices during the 1950s. Air raid sirens were erected around every American city as part of the civil defense program. Drills were held periodically. The very loud sirens were set off and people had to clear the streets.

Many buildings were designated as bomb shelters—usually on the first floor or in the basement of strongly built buildings. A yellow-and-black circle marked the buildings designated as public bomb shelters.

When air raid drills were conducted during school hours, children were instructed to get on the floor under their desks and away from any windows.

Some people built a bomb shelter on their property for their family. They dug a deep and wide hole as the foundation of a finished room. It was like the tornado shelters found in the Midwest.

There definitely was a fear of atomic war during the 1950s. Fortunately for all of us, it never happened.

SPUTNIK

IT WAS A COLD OCTOBER evening in 1957. My buddies and I were walking home from junior high basketball practice. The clear sky looked different to us that night.

Earlier that day we had learned the Soviet Union had launched the first satellite into orbit in outer space. We knew little about the space competition between the United States and Russia. All we knew was the Russians now had an item that was circling the earth, watching everything we did.

That was incredibly scary! It felt like all the science fiction movies we had seen about space and space travel had suddenly become real. We did not know to what extent the Russians were able to use the satellite. We just worried that it was only the first with more to come.

My friends and I hurried home to see if there was anything on television that would put our fears to rest. Unfortunately, TV was very limited in news coverage in those days.

That day changed everything for years to come. Luckily, our country met the challenge and was the first to land an astronaut on the moon.

But Neil Armstrong walking on the moon in 1969 was so many years off. In 1957, *Sputnik* terrified this preteen boy. I sure didn't sleep well that night.

BROOKLYN DODGERS

I OFFICIALLY BECAME A BASEBALL fan in 1952 at the age of seven. I was in second grade and heard about the World Series. Suddenly, I was very interested. It was early October, and everybody in the neighborhood was talking about the New York Yankees. Don't forget most of our neighbors, like my family, were people of Italian descent. They were all fans of the New York Yankees.

Why? Mostly because we idolized Joe DiMaggio, the great center-fielder on the Yankees during the 1940s. Among the best who ever played the game, Joe D. was of Italian descent. Everybody loved and respected him. DiMaggio had retired by the time the Yankees were playing in the World Series of 1952, but there were still many ballplayers on the team of Italian descent. Yogi Berra, Billy Martin, and Phil Rizzuto had led them to the 1952 World Series.

I was never one to follow the crowd and always rooted for the underdog. Everyone had a Lionel train, and I had an American Flyer train. Everyone rode a Schwinn bike, and I had a J.C. Higgins model.

So to go my own way, I bet my dad the Brooklyn Dodgers would beat the Yankees in the World Series. We put 25 cents on the series, and my Dodgers lost in six games. One year later, the Dodgers and the Yankees faced off again in the World Series. Once more, I bet 25 cents on the Dodgers, and once more they lost, although the Yanks needed seven games to finish them off.

I guess losing those bets to Dad and the misery I felt strengthened my commitment. You see, I began following the Brooklyn Dodgers faithfully every day. The newspapers and radio constantly promoted baseball during the 1950s. Back then, fans also had *The Sporting News*, the best baseball journal ever. By the late 1950s, I was a loyal subscriber.

Meanwhile, I was listening to Brooklyn Dodger radio broadcasts, especially in the evenings, when the New York stations would have better reception. Red Barber was the first Dodger broadcaster I listened to. He had a young assistant broadcaster by the name of Vin Scully. We all know Vin Scully's history with the Dodgers. I consider Vinnie one of the greatest, absolutely my favorite play-by-play baseball announcers.

I followed the Dodgers while they were still in Brooklyn. The "Boys of Summer" were all great players. Gil Hodges, Jim Gilliam, Pee Wee Reese, Jackie Robinson, Roy Campanella, Don Newcombe, Carl Furillo, Carl Erskine, Preacher Roe, Clem Labine, Johnny Podres, and Duke Snider, my favorite Dodger of all time.

In case you might have forgotten, Snider was one of three fantastic center fielders playing in New York at the same time during the 1950s. The other two were Mickey Mantle of the New York Yankees and Willie Mays of the New York Giants. "Willie, Mickey, and the Duke."

The 1954 World Series was played between the New York Giants and the Cleveland Indians. The Giants beat in four straight games a great Cleveland team that had won 116 games. I remember that World Series very well. I saved 25 cents by rooting for the Indians to beat the Giants, who were archrivals of my Brooklyn "Bums."

Redemption came at last in 1955. The Dodgers were back in the World Series, and beat the Yankees in seven games to become World Champions of baseball.

I was sad when the Dodgers left Brooklyn after the 1957 season to move to Los Angeles. However, my love for the team didn't diminish.

I was able to hear more ballgames since there was now a three-hour difference in time. Better, all the radio broadcasts were more powerful at night. I spent many nights listening to the Dodgers over my transistor radio while I was supposed to be asleep.

I am a Dodger to this day. As proof, let me say I named by black Labrador "Dodger Blue."

Baseball in the 1950s was the best ever. There were only eight teams in each league, so the talent was not watered down. Only the best players made the big leagues then.

By then, as you know, the racial barrier had been shattered. Many talented black players were playing in the 1950s, which wasn't the case before 1947.

The minor league systems owned by major league teams were filled with superb players waiting to get "the call" to the big leagues.

Baseball was truly our national pastime.

LITTLE LEAGUE BASEBALL

LITTLE LEAGUE BASEBALL, WHICH WAS launched elsewhere in Pennsylvania in the late 1930s, came to our town in the 1950s. One team was established in each of the eight wards, and parents were in charge of the teams, each having a manager.

All the boys in each ward between ages 8 and 12 were invited to try out for the Little League team there. Many kids tried out, but only a very few were chosen.

The games tended to be played in the evening, after dads had come home from work. Parents and other volunteers worked together to develop a beautiful ballpark next to the field where we used to play. The ballpark featured bleachers, dugouts, a grass infield, a scoreboard, and lights. Each team had its own uniforms, which was a pretty big deal.

1955 | Little league days. Lou with dad in back yard.

I played for the team in the fourth ward as a catcher. I was good and so was able to get a lot of playing time. Looking back, I can say I enjoyed playing Little League baseball. But I had much more fun playing "sandlot baseball" during the summer.

Only kids were involved—no parents. We managed to play very competitive baseball during those months. Two or three of the bigger guys chose their teams from everyone there. Everybody got to play, and we followed the rules of baseball.

We played round-robin tournaments all day. It was great fun with tremendous camaraderie. I couldn't wait to start playing every day.

On really hot days, we played baseball from early morning to the middle of the afternoon. Then we went swimming in the nearest pond or creek.

These days will never be forgotten.

PEANUTS AND CRACKER JACKS

"Take me out to the ball game.
Take me out with the crowd.
Buy me some peanuts and crackerjacks.
I don't care if I never get back."

THESE WORDS COME FROM THE famous Tin Pan Alley song *Take Me Out to the Ball Game*. They capture the excitement and fun a young boy like me felt about Major League Baseball during the golden days of the 1950s.

I grew up in New Castle in the western part of Pennsylvania. Our town was 60 miles north of Pittsburgh and 90 miles west of Cleveland. Both of those great had—and still have—baseball teams. The Pittsburgh Pirates played in the National League, while the Cleveland Indians belonged to the American League.

My earliest memories of Major League Baseball take me back to attending Pirates games in the early 1950s with my father and his friends. The Pirates called Forbes Field their home.

Ralph Kiner of the Pirates was my first baseball hero. He was the home run king of the National League in those years.

Other than Kiner, the hapless Pirates didn't give us much to cheer about in the early 1950s. So what? Like all my pals, I still loved to go to the games and rooted for the Pirates. Unless they were playing my favorite team, the Brooklyn Dodgers.

Forbes Field was old and had a lot of poles that blocked the view of many seats. We often sat in the bleachers, where a seat cost only 50 cents.

Baseball excursions were popular in the '50s. Local groups bought a bloc of tickets and sponsored a bus trip from our town to the games.

I liked to go on the trips sponsored by our Little League teams. On those days Little Leaguers were welcome to sit in the right-field stands as long as they were dressed in their uniforms.

It was neat to see the various teams from all across western Pennsylvania attending the game together with their coaches. Every time a ball was headed toward the right-field stands, hundreds of gloves would pop up trying to catch the fly ball.

Some excursions included games over in Cleveland. The Indians played at Municipal Stadium along Lake Erie. It was slightly newer than Forbes Field and could accommodate many more fans. The best trips to Cleveland featured a Sunday doubleheader when the New York Yankees came to visit. Remember, New Castle had lots of Yankee fans, thanks to Joe DiMaggio, Phil Rizzuto, Yogi Berra, and the other stars of Italian descent.

I loved the Cleveland excursions because usually they traveled from New Castle by train. To me the train ride was just as much fun as the baseball game. The train departed from the Baltimore & Ohio station on the west side of New Castle. It arrived at Municipal Stadium, with the tracks right next to the entrance. The train ride usually took two and a half hours except when there were delays. It always left early so we arrived on time for the game.

It was always great to see the American League stars when we went to Cleveland.

On Father's Day, St. Vitus Catholic Church often sponsored a father-and-son baseball trip. Dad and I would attend early Mass and then line up in front of the church. We formed a procession in the street, which was temporarily blocked off for about twelve blocks to the train station on the west side. The local Red Coat Band accompanied the procession, along with the priests and our Holy Name banner. All the fathers and sons were proud to make that march. I know I was.

We then boarded the train, which included delicious refreshments on the trip.

I loved to go to Major League Baseball games back in the day. More times I will never forget.

BASEBALL CARDS

SPRING WAS ALWAYS SPECIAL FOR kids back in the day. That was when all the corner stores and newsstands began selling baseball cards for that year. Two major companies produced baseball cards: Topps and Bowman. Sure, other companies made cards, but none of us collected them.

My favorite company was Topps. Their cards seemed to be more colorful. However, the set Bowman put out in 1955 stood out because each card put the color photograph of a ballplayer inside what was obviously wooden TV set. What we called "TV cards" seemed pretty neat to me.

Every baseball card came with a nice color photograph of the player in his uniform on the front. The back of the card contained the player's statistics plus a trivia question. The cards were individually packed in colorful waxed paper. One card including a flat piece of bubblegum cost one cent. There were five-card packs selling for 5 cents each.

It seemed like everyone collected baseball cards. We rode our bikes all over town to find stores that carried the latest series of cards released periodically through the summer.

Card companies also supplied checklists to encourage us to to collect the entire set, which was distributed in five or six series of cards. A complete set contained anywhere from 300 to 400 individual cards.

Collecting cards involved other activities. Each of us trying to get all the cards in a series ended up with hundreds of duplicate cards. So we traded cards with each other to get ones we didn't have.

Kids also stuck duplicate cards in the spokes of our bicycles with a clothespin to achieve a motor-like sound. Card companies didn't design their baseball cards for that purpose, but invented it to make bike riding a lot more fun.

Of course, the main activity we did with our baseball cards was "flipping." You would hold a card at your waist and flip it toward the ground so it landed on its face or its back. This was termed "heads or tails." Flipping was an early form of gambling we learned thanks to our baseball cards.

How did the game work? One guy would flip five to ten cards on the ground. A certain number of heads and a certain number of tails resulted. If the other fellow playing matched the number of heads and tails on the ground, he was entitled to all the cards. But if he didn't match the number of heads and tails on the ground, the first player won the event. Victory entitled him to all the cards.

We would flip cards for hours. At the end of the day, we counted how many cards we had won or lost.

Years later, when the market for baseball cards exploded about the time the market for toy trains did, we learned an unfortunate truth. Flipping ruined the condition of many of our cards, and they were worthless in later years.

Needless to say, any cards that survived from being in our bicycle spokes were worth nothing. But no amount of money could replace all the fun we had playing with our cards.

Back in the 1950s, all of us became very knowledgeable about the game of baseball because we read the back of the baseball cards. And just think of how our reading skills improved! Yes, we were all students of the game. Baseball was our true "National Pastime."

NEW CARS

ASK ANYBODY WHO CAME OF age in the 1950s, including me, and you'll probably hear the same opinion of American automobiles from that era. Namely, no other decade saw as many advances in their production and technology.

After World War II, Americans became very mobile. The national highway system was beginning to reach more distant areas with better, smoother roads in the entire country. Besides getting jobs and making babies, the soldiers and sailors coming home from the war were buying homes and automobiles. Cars became the major mode of transportation. Cars unquestionably made America move.

Automobiles and the magic they conveyed captivated young boys in every corner of the country. New cars were developed and introduced each year, and we couldn't wait to see them. The new models entranced us, even though most of us weren't old enough to drive.

September marked the introduction of the new models. We couldn't wait to see what the "Big Three" automakers were going to bring out. Back then, General Motors, Ford Motor Company, and Chrysler represented the three giants of the automotive industry in America. Next in line was American Motors. Then there were the minor players—Hudson, Nash, Packard, and Studebaker—most of which didn't last through the 1950s.

When September rolled around and the new models were due to arrive, dealerships in each town put paper over the large windows of their showrooms. That way no one could see the new cars until the big day when they were introduced to the community.

Every year, or so it seemed, the models were more futuristic. Cars were styled to look and feel like rocket ships, right down to their huge fins on the rear.

Best of all, cars produced in the 1950s were much more colorful than the ones made in the 1940s. Besides improved styling and dazzling colors the new models boasted more powerful motors. New technology enabled them to move faster and faster.

Cars from the 1950s were larger, heavier, and faster than those cars of the 1940s. What helped to take advantage of their speed was the fact that gasoline cost 25 cents a gallon.

In June 1953, General Motors introduced the Corvette, the first sports car in the Chevrolet line. All the young guys made it a favorite. Ford followed with its first sportscar, the Thunderbird in 1955.

What makes the first Thunderbird special to me is many years later, my older sister Anarose bought a red '55 in like-new condition. Lucky me, because she let me borrow her '55 T-bird to drive to my high school senior activities.

I do not have to tell you how great it felt to drive that beautiful red Thunderbird during that incredible week in June of 1962.

The technological changes improving American cars were nothing short of amazing. Cars got better every year in the 1950s, due to the intense competition between the major auto manufacturers.

Today, all the cars look alike and tend to be a lot smaller and less luxurious. In the 1950s, all of them had character, even the notorious Edsel.

USED CARS

THE DEMAND FOR AUTOMOBILES IN any shape and condition was booming in the 1950s. Besides the new models pouring off the automakers' assembly lines in Detroit, used cars were in high demand.

Many people who could not afford a new car priced on the lower side at $1,500 to $3,000 began to look for a good used one. Lots filled with used models soon popped up all over the city. The used cars were cleaned and displayed in small lots. Dealers lit up their lots with strings of bright bulbs to allow for night shopping.

What did the old Dodges and Buicks sell for? Guys brought home used cars for $500, but some bragged about paying as little as $100.

Sadly, many used-car dealers were not the most honest fellows. They had a lot of tricks to hide problems with the used cars they sold. They hoped offering a 30-day warranty would be enough to get any car out of the lot.

To be fair, plenty of honest and fair people sold used cars. They later moved up to become reputable dealers in brand-new cars.

Our corner used-car dealer was located at the intersection of Pearson and Taylor Streets. As I remember, Taylor was not a residential street. There were eight used-car lots within a four-block area.

I spent a lot of time hanging around the used-car lots and picking up odd jobs. Frankly, I got a real education from the owners and the used-car salesmen.

Their selling philosophy boiled down to a simple motto. They would "detail to retail" their used cars. These guys were characters who taught me a lot—some good and some not so good.

ELVIS

ON THE EVENING OF SUNDAY, September 9, 1956, my world changed. Like millions of other kids across America, I first saw Elvis Presley. Not in person, but in our living room on our family's black-and-white TV. Elvis appeared on *The Ed Sullivan Show*.

I have to be honest and say I was not a real Elvis fan at first. I wasn't crazy about all that shaking around and girl screaming. I thought he was a fad and would soon be forgotten. But what did a 12-year-old boy in sixth grade know anyway? At the time, the music I preferred was what we called doo-wop.

Soon, Elvis Presley became the "King of Rock and Roll." He released so many hit single records. I came to like more and more of them, but honestly did not realize how great an entertainer Elvis was until many years had passed.

These days I consider myself an avid Elvis fan. The world of music lost so much when he died at a young age in August 1977. That was about 20 years after his final appearance on *The Ed Sullivan Show* in January of 1957. When I think of Elvis, I remember the millions of records he sold and the many movies he made in the 1950s and '60s. Later, of course, his performances, especially in Las Vegas, were legendary.

During the 1950s, as I mentioned, my friends and I preferred the groups and singers that performed blues and doo-wop music. A few years later, the Beatles won my allegiance. And I still enjoy their music.

Another favorite from the 1950s was Buddy Holly and his group, the Crickets. Sad to recall how he died in an airplane crash at the age of 22 in February of 1959. Buddy Holly's death is referred to as "The day the music died" in the song *American Pie* written and sung by Don McClain in 1971.

JAMES DEAN

IN THE 1950s, MOVIES INTRODUCED us to a new phenomenon with teenagers. To point to one motion picture that changed things, I have to mention *Rebel Without a Cause* from 1955. It brought us an unforgettable new young actor named James Dean.

Rebel Without a Cause was about urban and suburban adolescents rebelling against their parents and the rules of society. Movies like it caught on with kids of that era, and they started to emulate the rebellious nature of the teenagers they saw in those movies. Boys bought black leather jackets like the type Marlon Brando wore in the movie, *The Wild One*. Released in 1953, it was about motorcycles and rebellious adolescents. Kids also changed their hairstyles to copy what they saw in these movies. Boys wore their hair much longer and slicked back with heavy creams and grease. We called the boys who wore their hair that way "greasers."

The sides were also long and combed back to the rear where each side would meet in the middle of the back of their head in a straight line. We called that style a "DA," initials that stood for "Duck's Ass." The hairstyle also included a "spit curl" on the front forehead.

Our parents refused to pay for leather jackets so we could follow with what they criticized as "this foolishness." When we were cold, they bought us a navy blue wool pea coat, and that was that.

That didn't stop us from trying. We bought lightweight black corduroy jackets. They were less expensive than leather jackets.

My pals and I formed groups, clubs, or gangs with individual names for each group. "Angels" and "East Side Tigers" were two of the names of gangs I remember. Then we sewed the name on the back of our jacket with white felt letters.

Now we could walk around with pride. We felt we were showing group solidarity while rebelling against all grownups.

Looking back, I can say the gang stage is normal for adolescent boys and does little harm. We attended movies, taking up one or two rows all dressed alike. That was really cool.

Too bad James Dean died after he made *Rebel Without a Cause* and two other movies. It would've been interesting to see what he might have accomplished in his future years.

Many other movies influenced the large population of baby boomer adolescents. I think of *Blackboard Jungle* from 1955 and *Rock Around the Clock* from 1956 as two movies that fueled young boys and girls so long ago.

Hollywood was making money from this new group of teens. And those movies were certainly not making it easier for their parents.

POLITICS

KIDS IN THE 1950s DID not care about politics. However, I remember getting a taste of politics while hanging around my parents' corner store.

Dad worked there in the evenings, and many of his buddies would come in to talk about municipal politics. Things could get loud whenever they started discussing (and arguing about) various local issues.

Dad was a Franklin Roosevelt Democrat. He always gave President Roosevelt credit for ending the Great Depression. Dad boasted about FDR being the only person ever elected to the presidency for four terms.

I learned a lot by listening to the different positions the fellas would take. And I recall how excited many of them felt when, at the end of the 1950s, a new young senator was nominated to run for president. His name was Kennedy.

PART 2:
I Still Haven't Met a Train I Didn't Like

ESSAYS FROM 2014

by Lou Palumbo

FOR LOVE OR FOR MONEY
PEOPLE VALUE THEIR TOY TRAINS FOR DIFFERENT REASONS

I OFTEN WONDER WHY SO many people are so adamant about collecting toy trains. Is it for the love of trains, or is it for the money they are convinced they can gain by collecting them?

Let's look at the majority of the folks collecting miniature trains.

Most of the people in the hobby today started collecting trains when they were kids—probably in the 1940s and '50s. Some collectors are older and some are younger, but most fall in the "baby boomer" category. Whatever their age, it's also likely their parents provided that first train, and the love of toy trains began. Those toy trains usually were the only trains most collectors owned until many years later. They were adults when they rediscovered the hobby of collecting toy trains.

We all experience this yearning to remember younger days, when everything seemed safe at home. Warm feelings of returning to a cherished past are what the love of toy trains is all about for me. This is the reason I've been involved in the hobby for my entire life, and why I've been seriously collecting since the 1970s.

In addition, human beings are, by nature, born collectors. Therefore, it's safe to say the excitement provided by the hunt, along with the thrill ignited by the find, also fuel the train hobby. Each time any of us attend a train show or visit a hobby shop we embark on an adventure, one that holds the possibility of making a new find.

Now let's consider another important aspect of the toy train hobby. I'm referring here to the monetary and not the emotional value of vintage trains.

Somewhere along the trail of the search for trains many collectors become obsessed with their value. They spend a lot of time worrying about the trains' cost at the time of their purchase compared to the current value. They justify the money spent on this hobby as an investment.

As a long-time collector and the owner of a thriving toy train store, I think I have the expertise and the experience to comment knowledgeably on this approach. I strongly recommend against it. In today's market, toy trains should be purchased for the enjoyment to be derived from them and not as an investment.

Buying and selling toy trains as a business—and not an investment—is an entirely different matter. Since the 1980s, a number of collectors have tried to turn their hobby into a full-time business. I count myself among them.

However, the landscape in the hobby has changed dramatically in the past 10 or so years and is very different from what it was in the 1980s. To be sure, some hobbyists were fortunate enough and worked hard enough to develop great shops and to succeed as train dealers.

The guys making the transition from collectors to dealers tended to be good business people who realized they could no longer approach their love of vintage trains as a hobby. It had to be treated as a business, and they focused on making a profit—as well they should.

There are still some guys who love trains and sell them to support their hobby. They gather trains wherever they can and bring them to the market so other people can enjoy them. This description fits my business.

Whatever your approach to the hobby, we can all agree toy trains provide lots of enjoyment. This is a great hobby whether it's for love or money.

Keep searchin'

LIONEL'S FAUX SALE

RESTORATIONS HAVE AN IMPORTANT PLACE IN OUR HOBBY

RECENTLY I RECEIVED AN EMAIL from Kenneth Kadzielawski, a *Classic Toy Trains* reader who enjoys "Views From The Underground." He reminded me that in February of 2014 we'll celebrate the golden anniversary of a monumental cultural event. Yes, 50 years ago, on February 9, 1964, the Beatles first appeared in America on *The Ed Sullivan Show*.

Kenneth detailed his love for the Beatles and described his collections of GI Joe action figures and Lionel trains. He signed off as "A sixty-year-old Beatles fan, who still plays with trains."

The email I received from Kenneth made me think of another "Beatles fan" of about the same age who is also very involved in toy trains.

I'm talking about Len Carparelli, a renowned restoration artist for toy trains and longtime contributor to CTT. In case you didn't know it, Len also plays guitar for Beatles Faux Sale, a great Beatles tribute band that performs in New York and other cities along the East Coast. Len portrays George Harrison.

In the world of toy trains, Len is best known for his beautiful restorations of Lionel postwar F3 diesels. The most popular of which, to no one's surprise, are the Santa Fe models painted in the famous red-and-silver "warbonnet" scheme.

Len, who also does other postwar and prewar trains, takes pride in his superb screen-printing techniques. Using them and his decades of skill, he can repaint a shell or refinish an entire locomotive, including the frame and motor. He is also able to enhance engines with minor flaws. When finished, his restorations have a beauty rivaling that of original Lionel models in mint condition.

Restorations and repaints were very popular from the 1970s into the 1990s. Operators were picking up postwar locomotives in average or poor condition and having them professionally repainted by craftsmen like Len. Most of those restored engines ended up running on O gauge layouts. Collectors who could not find or afford mint or like-new originals might choose to display them

Either way, only a handful of people had enough talent to create masterful reproductions. As a consequence, those individuals received many projects. Their backlog grew until the customers might have to wait six, nine, or even twelve months. Typical prices charged to have a pair of Lionel F3s completely restored, including frames, motors, and body shells ranged from $300 all the way up to $500.

Like everything else in the toy train hobby, the place of restorations has changed. Lionel started to aggressively improve the postwar remakes with the introduction of its Postwar Celebration Series in the first years of the 21st century. The company has added some really some beautiful items to the popular series.

Williams by Bachmann also started to produce very nice copies of Lionel locomotives from the 1950s with its Golden Memories Edition. Those O gauge engines look sharp and run well, and are less expensive than the other remakes.

Today's operators, eager to run postwar locomotives, express satisfaction with the reissues from Lionel and Williams. Collectors, however, still want original items. They maintain the market for old engines restored in the U.S. That proves fortunate for Len and the dwindling number of restoration artists. Demand for their work remains strong, and they have lots of projects. This proves my point that in business "there's room for everybody."

Here's to the Beatles and toy trains—May they live forever in our hearts!

Keep searchin'

LIVING IN A "THROW-AWAY SOCIETY"

HOW MODERN CONSUMING HABITS AFFECT TOY TRAINS

WINTER REMINDS ME OF THE many evenings in the 1980s when I was repairing the prewar and postwar locomotives folks had brought to my store or I had purchased. Lionel and American Flyer engines were durable and inexpensive to repair or restore, so the projects went smoothly.

During the holiday season I usually would sell every steam engine I had in stock. Locomotives equipped with smoke and whistles were the most popular. Postwar engines provided a better alternative to the locomotives produced for the Lionel line in the 1970s and early '80s.

To prepare for each train season I would buy a large supply of "Electric Reverse Unit" (better known as E-units) drums, fingers, and spools of soft wire. I also had to purchase loads of other Lionel parts, especially brushes and smoke unit components.

Repairs went on all the time. Today, though, the business of repairing vintage trains has declined significantly.

The production of trains improved during the 1980s and '90s. New companies, led by MTH Electric Trains, put on the market many beautiful and well-made trains resembling what had been released in the 1940s and '50s. Eventually, MTH offered replicas of many of the finest prewar engines and sets.

I can remember when we repaired radios with tubes sold in cases available at every five-and-ten-cent store. A tube could be tested and a suitable replacement easily and inexpensively purchased. Televisions, washing machines, and any kind of appliance were all repaired in the 1950s and '60s.

Today, these items including computers and other electronic gadgets are routinely thrown away when they no longer function. Why? We're told they are too expensive to fix, and we are instructed to buy a new unit.

I'm not sure what this frame of mind means to the American economy. Maybe it helps industries and retailers. Somehow, though, it seems wrong to me.

Toy trains seem to be heading in the same direction. The latest models have many fancy features that lure buyers into making major purchases. For their money consumers bring home locomotives with great sound systems and amazing detail. These days operators can run multiple trains using command control systems.

Old O and S gauge trains are no longer the only show in the town. As a result, they have been pushed into the background.

There's a trade-off when products displace old ones. The new, superior looking and operating models can be expensive to repair if an electronic component fails. Also, it can be difficult to find replacement parts for some relatively new trains and accessories.

So, what do we do with these models when they develop problems? Many hobbyists are waiting impatiently for someone to develop cost-effective repair methods for their sidelined locomotive.

Look, I also enjoy all the new products and gadgets and don't want to revert back to the old TV sets and other items that make our life less easy or less enjoyable to live. But we pay a price when we forget how to repair and reuse old trains. This is the reason I maintain my skills and go on repairing vintage models with Lionel's reliable smoke and whistle and Flyer's dependable "choo-choo" sound.

Keep searchin'

27 YEARS AND STILL ROLLING
NEARLY THREE DECADES OF LOOKING AT OUR HOBBY

FOLKS DON'T NORMALLY MAKE A big to-do about their 27th anniversary. But celebrating my 27 years of writing the "Views from the Underground" column takes on importance because I'm marking the occasion in a unique way. I've gathered these dozens of essays and put them together in a new book. It's one I think every reader of *Classic Toy Trains* will treasure.

The first "Views from the Underground" appeared in the initial issue of *Train Traders*, a publication put out for train collectors by my friend and fellow hobbyist, Bill Brown. He resides in my hometown of New Castle, Pa., which is where I had opened the Underground Railroad Shoppe. Bill asked me to share my thoughts on the hobby, and I became a regular contributor to *Train Traders*. Since the name of my store made a point of the fact that visitors had to walk down a flight of stairs to reach it, I decided to call my column "Views from the Underground."

Among the hobby insiders reading "Views from the Underground" was Tom McComas, already publishing books about Lionel trains and producing videos of toy trains. Tom launched *Toy Train Review Journal* in the early 1990s and requested I write for it. He included other essays I wrote in the price guides published by TM Books & Video.

My goal has been to share with longtime hobbyists and newcomers my experiences as a collector and dealer in this hobby and the insights I have acquired. I do so in an informal style packed with homespun humor. My two favorite words describing the columns are "enjoyable" and "informative."

Over the past 27 years I've emphasized different facets of life—mostly positive yet all related to collecting of toy trains. In addition, I make an effort to examine the characteristics of the people who collect them.

I have fun describing my generation: the so-called "Baby Boomers." They make up the largest portion of toy train collectors.

Issues and good times are unlimited in the hobby. Every day something comes to my attention that generates another column.

I started writing "Views from the Underground" for *Classic Toy Trains* in 2007. Many subjects are covered relating to collecting and enjoying toy trains. The stories are timeless and are very enjoyable to reread.

Andy Rooney was a favorite author of mine. I liked the short essays he read at the end of each *60 Minutes* television show. His stories were entertaining and informative—there go those two great words again!

Knowing how much I like reading the books containing collections of Rooney's short essays, I decided about a year ago to see if I could do the same.

That's what I have done. You can now pick up a copy of my new book, *I Never Met a Train I Didn't Like: The Art and Enjoyment of Collecting Toy Trains*. This paperback publication includes all of my past columns, along with a terrific biographical foreword written by CTT Senior Editor Roger Carp.

I've been fortunate to meet many of the people who read "Views from the Underground." Also, I have received letters and emails from them and encountered a lot of them at my store or train meets. Their comments guide me in obtaining topics, concerns, and information for future columns.

Now I'm hoping this collection of essays and stories will inspire hobbyists to enjoy their toy trains. Better yet, I hope what I've written since June 1987 will help all the new people getting into the greatest of hobbies.

I've had a real blast sharing what I've observed and learned with our extended toy train family. Now I'm looking forward to doing so for another 27 years!

Keep searchin'

I'VE SEEN FIRE!

CONFRONTING EVERY HOBBYIST'S WORST NIGHTMARE

AMONG THE MANY GREAT ARTICLES in the March 2014 issue of *Classic Toy Trains* was one that brought chills to me. Roger Carp's story about O gauge operator Frank Battaglia and the house fire that destroyed an earlier layout built by Frank brought back unpleasant memories. The article also made me reflect on what I learned from a terrible experience.

Frank described to Roger how much he lost because of a fire at his home years ago. What I read in the article sure struck a chord with me.

On March 4, 1988, my toy train store and pride and joy—the Underground Railroad Shoppe in New Castle, Pa.—suffered heavy losses due to a fire. As was my practice, I kept the store open until 9 o'clock. The guy who helped with chores had left. Meanwhile, I was packing for a train show in Cleveland I planned to attend the following day.

During that night I had been restoring a bunch of Lionel no. 022 remote-controlled switches. I usually repaired them so they worked well. I had finished sanding the switches in anticipation of repainting all the bases. I must have had about 20 pairs of switches I was going to bring to the show.

I was painting the switches in a room off the hallway between my showroom and the room where I had an O gauge layout. By the way, you can read about the latest version of that display in the November 2013 CTT.

The room also served as a place to store Large scale sets, which I stacked on high wood shelves. I lined the switches on the lower shelves and sprayed a coat of black enamel paint on them. I would return to the room periodically to give them additional coats as they dried until they were covered.

While waiting for each coat of paint to dry I resumed packing trains. I had been doing this for about an hour when I heard a loud pop in the repair room. I dashed back there and flung open the door only to be met with a burst of heat and fire. Dark orange flames had lit up everything in sight, and thick black smoke poured out of the door and filled the hallway with dangerous fumes.

I ran to a telephone. I had to get through to the local fire department. Sad to say, our town did not at the time have 911 or emergency capability. Instead, I had to fumble through my directory to get the department's phone number. Failing to do so, I raced outside and did reach the fire fighters.

Those brave men saved the building. Too bad the flames and smoke damaged almost all the contents of my store. The heat ended up melting the layout. Nothing could be salvaged. Of course, what the smoke and heat didn't ruin was destroyed by the water poured on the scene.

Fire inspectors found that Styrofoam protecting components of the Large scale sets was the source of the heat and smoke. Needless to say, the fire was a sad and depressing episode in my life. O and S gauge treasures collected over many years were lost. Pieces of trains and railroad memorabilia suddenly melted into unidentifiable blobs of plastic and metal. Thousands of dollars worth of parts and hard-to-find trains ended up being shoveled into garbage cans from the wet, ash-filled floors.

Sorting through the rubble reminded me of news clips shown during times of war and disaster. Fortunately, no lives were lost there. Meanwhile, my plans for the store seemed to have gone up in smoke. I had only enough insurance to cover a fraction of the replacement cost for the collectible trains I lost.

Like Frank Battaglia, I had to decide whether to go on. In my case, that meant rebuild the store or close it forever. I'll continue my story in the next CTT.

Keep searchin'

...AND I'VE SEEN RAIN
COMING BACK STRONG AFTER A DEVASTATING FIRE

IN THE JULY ISSUE OF *Classic Toy Trains* I described a terrible fire that had all but ruined my store, the Underground Railroad Shoppe, more than 20 years ago. I wrote about the fears I experienced after losing inventory and a layout I had built as a labor of love. I even wondered how I would come back from the fire.

Here, I plan to tell you how I did just that—how after seeing fire and then the accompanying sadness and worry (what you could call the "rain") I managed to rekindle (no pun intended) my enthusiasm for the hobby. From there, it was just a matter of time and effort before the store and I were back.

Looking back, I will never forget the initial impact I felt when a couple of our town's firemen led me back into the store after they had put out the fire. Naturally, everything was dark. The electricity was off, and the only light we had came from flashlights.

The main area looked like a haunted house at an amusement park. Everything was black and covered with a heavy dark film. All the trains on shelves had melted into a macabre stream of plastic running into each other down to the lower shelves in a frozen waterfall of pain.

Although the flames never reached the show room, the heat generated from the fire in the repair room containing the sets filled with Styrofoam melted everything made of plastic. The heavy black smoke did the rest of the damage.

In addition to seeing all the damage, I smelled the dreadful odor of a building fire. That stench truly assaulted all of my senses.

Of course, the water used to extinguish the fire had also wreaked its own kind of devastation. Wading through six inches of black, ash-filled water I couldn't remember ever feeling as depressed and hurt in my life. The future looked bleak, and I wondered whether I would ever be able to restore my little train shop.

The next day did nothing to revive my hope. Returning to the store, I was hit with the pungent fire odor. Meanwhile, workers were shoveling the damaged trains and parts into barrels to be thrown out.

Sure, I had insurance. Unfortunately, I had only enough to cover about a quarter of my loss. If I wanted to rebuild the Underground Railroad Shoppe and my dreams, I had no choice but to start with little. Good thing I was young at the time (43 years old) and had the encouragement of my family.

Friends and customers were supportive, too. Some volunteered to help with the cleanup. With their help and kindness, we moved ahead. Before long, I had a sale of salvaged items, putting them on tables in our parking lot. Many people attended, and it helped me buy new product to restock the store. It took a lot of work, but the shop was ready for the Christmas season. With the help of friends, I rebuilt the O gauge layout. As you learned from an article in the November 2013 issue of CTT, we add to it each year.

In retrospect, I can pass along two nuggets of wisdom I learned the hard way. First, buy as much insurance as you can afford. Second, never spray-paint anything indoors unless you have good ventilation in an up-to-date paint booth. I know fellas who still paint models in their basement, not far from a hot-water heater. Listen to me—that is a recipe for a horrible disaster!

I'm grateful to have survived the fire and thankful no one was injured. We were able to continue with the shop and share the hobby with many people.

My greatest dream was rebuilt, and I continue to live it every day.

Keep searchin'

RENEWED APPRECIATION FOR "FLYER GUYS"
REVISITING A COLUMN ABOUT
AMERICAN FLYER ENTHUSIASTS

REMEMBER HOW, BACK IN THE July 2009 issue of *Classic Toy Trains*, the topic of my "Views from the Underground" was "Flyer guys?" Well, as I have discovered in the five years since that column was published, I really hit a nerve with a number of readers who collect or operate American Flyer S gauge trains.

Let me summarize what I had written. Early in 2009, there was an auction of several rare items that had once belonged to A.C. Gilbert Co., the founder of the business that made American Flyer trains during the late prewar and then the postwar eras. I attended that event and thought some of the Flyer enthusiasts there were a bit intolerant of my wearing a Lionel jacket.

Based on that experience, as well as others in my four decades in hobby, I wrote, "Lionel enthusiasts tend to tolerate Flyer guys. Too bad the opposite generally isn't the case!" S gauge hobbyists "never fail to express their dislike of Lionel's 'unrealistic' three-rail O gauge track and non-scale trains." I noted that even though the war between the two sides has yet to end, Lionel won that contest by sheer numbers and the quality, selection, and beauty of its trains.

As I say, complaints about the tone of the article and how it cast a negative light on Flyer collectors erupted. Frankly, I've never heard the end of the issue.

Recently I discussed the article with Dennis Cannon. He's a good friend, a member of the Train Collectors Association, and a self-proclaimed "American Flyer collector extraordinaire." Dennis attended the same auction and criticized me for focusing on a few of the other Flyer enthusiasts at the auction rather than the rare items, including furniture and paintings from Gilbert's office and engineering drawings.

Good point—except that column was not intended to inform CTT readers about the auction. I'm not a reporter covering major events in the toy train hobby. The editors of the magazine want me to offer commentary about trends, past and present, as I see them and to explain their importance and impact.

Therefore, my remarks about the auction were intended to lead into a discussion of some of the general characteristics I've noticed of many of the American Flyer enthusiasts I have met at hobby shows and conventions and at my train store.

In that column I aimed to demonstrate the unusual pride and loyalty most "Flyer guys" have for their S gauge trains and accessories. As I went on, I seldom see the same kind of loyalty in Lionel collectors. I also wrote about how American Flyer S gauge was more realistic then Lionel O gauge, which might be the reason the smaller trains seemed to look better on layouts.

One more point to consider. I always write to inform and entertain. I was trying to describe Flyer guys with a little humor. However, if anyone took my comments the wrong way and thought I was being sarcastic or disrespectful, well, all I can do right now is apologize and again express my love of all toy trains.

So, from one "Flyer guy" to Dennis and all the other ones out there who are reading CTT, I'll sign off this month with two bits of wisdom. First, as I titled my recent book, *I Never Met a Train I Didn't Like*. Second, Flyer Forever!

Keep searchin'

"SHOWROOMING"
INTRODUCING THE LATEST PHENOMENON IN RETAIL SALES

THE UNDERGROUND RAILROAD SHOPPE OPENED in New Castle, Pa., in 1985. You do the math—my store is about to enter its 30th holiday season.

I've had many great experiences over the past 29 years. As important, I have learned a lot about what it means to own your own retail business.

One of my pet peeves during the early years related to when a customer would walk in and read one of the copies of *Model Railroader* magazine on my counter. He was searching for prices advertised by the large national train distributors so he could compare them with what I was charging at my store.

The inventory in my store has changed over the past 30 years. Initially, I carried mostly postwar and prewar toy trains. Only about 10 percent of my inventory was brand-new Lionel products.

Now our inventory consists mainly of new products from all the major toy train manufacturers as well as a complete line of accessories for the train hobby. We also sell more new and like-new preowned trains, many of which I purchased from collectors. The selection of postwar and prewar trains is much smaller now.

A new practice has entered the retail business world that people refer to as "showrooming." This is when a customer uses a cell phone as a computer to shop online while reviewing items in a retail outlet like mine. Not many of my customers do this, but showrooming is definitely on the rise.

Do I hate showrooming? Do I protest when I see a customer doing this and ask him or her to quit or leave the premises? You may be surprised to learn that I do not. I have come to accept the practice, believing that price shopping is a good way to buy products. After all, people are always trying to get the best price and retailers like myself should be aware of that fact and quickly come to accept it.

I'm glad customers have driven to my store and are more than willing to give my staff and me opportunities to sell a product to them. Many times showrooming works to my advantage because it offers me a chance to match or even beat the best price a customer can find online.

Additionally, as my customers realize, they are able to see and test the product in the store. If they like it, they can buy it and take it home the same day.

When dealing with a small shop like mine, customers are able to form personal relationships with the management. Staff members can exchange information to meet the hobby needs of different customers.

I try to make a visit to the Underground Railroad Shoppe pleasant by filling it with train-related items and a large selection of old and new trains. During the holiday season we open an O gauge layout to the public (*Classic Toy Trains* showed that railroad in its November 2013 issue).

Browsing helps customers get new ideas. They also discover unexpected trains and other products and often end up buying something unfamiliar to them.

Generally, my staff and I can match prices advertised by online stores on the preordered new products of current train companies. Better yet, we sell service for many of the items customers buy at the shop.

Someone interested in a preowned train finds the art of negotiation is alive and well. We take trades on items offered for sale. You can't do that online!

More retailers should adopt this open attitude toward showrooming. Keep in mind, we would all like to see you in our stores during this holiday season!

Keep searchin'

HOLIDAY AROMAS AND TOY TRAINS
DIFFERENT SMELLS TRIGGER MANY GREAT MEMORIES

CAN YOU BELIEVE THAT ANOTHER year of enjoying our new and vintage toy trains is about over? Another year of seeing what current manufacturers have released and looking at the classics available in train stores and auction houses.

Every year ends with the holiday season, the perfect time for sharing the pleasures of our hobby with family and friends. Something you'll be sharing is the array of wonderful smells associated with this season and toy trains.

When I think back on growing up in the 1950s, I remember the new and delightful smells brought to my family's home during the Christmas season.

Everything started with Thanksgiving. I love thinking about how the smell of roast turkey woke me up on that Thursday morning. Then the smells of pumpkin pie and roasted chestnuts began dancing around the house.

A few weeks later, the aromas of freshly baked holiday cookies permeated our house. The smell of anise dominated as my mother baked pizzelles (traditional Italian waffle cookies) one by one with the iron pizzelle maker she held over the flame of her stove.

The next aroma came a week before Christmas when Dad brought a newly cut pine tree into our living room. The smell of pine remained long after December 25!

Dad set the tree up early so construction of my S gauge layout could begin. He and I used half the living room to set up my own American Flyer train with all my accessories. We would have used more space, but Mom never gave in on that request.

The next smell I associate with Christmas was the most memorable one. American Flyer smoke pouring out of the stack on my no. 290 steam locomotive soon filled the room with a cedar-like odor that was both familiar and comforting.

Flyer smoke came in a liquid form packed in red capsules with a nipple on one end. The capsule was filled with an oily liquid you accessed by sticking a needle in the nipple end and then squeezing into a funnel made to fit into the smokestack of any Flyer steamer. I thought that was neat.

My buddies who had Lionel trains got their steamers to smoke by inserting special pellets into the stack. The pills melted when they reached the heating element inside the smoke unit and then changed into smoke that puffed out.

Frankly, my Flyer engines smoked much better than their Lionel engines. In my opinion, the cedar smell was better than the smell of the Lionel smoke.

Another wonderful smell emitted by all electric trains was the ozone created when they were put on the track. I've since learned the unmistakable odor was produced when the carbon brushes on the small electric motors initially came in contact with the brush plate installed on the armature.

Christmas Eve always brought to our home the aroma of seafood and pasta. Since we did not eat meat on Christmas Eve, my mom prepared many types of fish to celebrate the festivities. The smell and food can never be forgotten.

Yes, the different aromas of holidays remain very special to my family and me. They revive memories of members who are no longer alive and who supported my love of toy trains, particularly my American Flyer roster and S gauge layout.

So let me now close by wishing all of you, Merry Christmas and Happy Holidays!

PART 2:
I Still Haven't Met a Train I Didn't Like

ESSAYS FROM 2015

CALLING FOR ACCESSORIES
WE NEED MORE INNOVATIVE AND INEXPENSIVE ACCESSORIES

OVER THE THIRTY YEARS I'VE owned a toy train store, I have sold many trains to people who are buying the first set for youngsters. They usually ask if they can add anything to that set. They have in mind another piece of rolling stock.

I tell them nothing makes a train come to life and increases its play value, especially for a child, like an operating accessory!

In recent decades, Lionel and MTH Electric Trains have reissued a number of classic accessories, especially those from the postwar era. They've updated mechanisms and substituted better motors to improve many popular freight-handling items and animated towers.

Both Lionel and MTH have also turned their attention to the S gauge accessories introduced by the A.C. Gilbert Co. for its American Flyer line. They have brought back some wonderful models, including my all-time favorite accessory, one I consider among the most reliable ever made: the oil drum loader nicknamed by Gilbert "Louie the Loader" (another reason I liked it!).

That accessory—identified as no. 779 in 1955-56 and no. 23779 in 1957-61—consisted of a small forklift type of vehicle on which perched the driver, a die-cast metal figure I always thought was my namesake, the hard-working Louie.

Everyone loves to watch the little guy move the drums from a waiting ramp on the platform. They roll down the ramp so they can be taken and moved to the waiting gondola on the other side of the ramp.

Lionel took a bold step by reproducing the oil drum loader for its American Flyer line in 1985 as the no. 2300; additional versions followed in the next decade. What's really neat about this accessory—traditionally associated with S gauge trains—is that it can easily be made compatible for O gauge trains.

This type of accessory should always be available. It's perfect! Sadly, Lionel no longer catalogs the oil drum loader.

Manufacturers need to develop new accessories that are as reliable as the oil drum loader yet will not break anyone's bank account. People who are getting started in the hobby and are trying to get kids involved need to be able to buy low-cost accessories to add to new starter sets.

I believe the price for a dependable and entertaining operating accessory should not exceed $125. After all, you can find O gauge starter sets priced at $125 to $275.

Accessories with lights and moving parts are favorites among new train buyers. Sadly, I can recall many nice operating accessories that were gone after being cataloged for a year or two.

Leading train manufacturers should produce a separate catalog every year that's filled with all the accessories they have recently made and sold well.

Many new buyers look at catalogs from recent years and then ask about buying an accessory they've just seen and read about. They are disappointed when they learn these accessories are no longer available.

Accessories fuel the hobby because they make playing with trains more fun to new and younger enthusiasts. Even those of us who have been in the hobby longer would be pleased to see a wider range of new and old items available year after year for us to install on our O or S gauge model railroads.

Let's hope manufacturers are moving in that direction in their research and development departments. No matter how long you've been enjoying your trains, you're always looking for something new to add.

Keep searchin'

STATE OF THE HOBBY

MORE RETIRED PEOPLE AND KIDS ARE ENJOYING TOY TRAINS

ONE THING I REMEMBER WELL from the economics courses I took in college is that supply and demand have impact on every market. I keep that fundamental principle in mind every day at the Underground Railroad Shoppe, the toy and model train retail outlet I own and manage in New Castle, Pa.

I'm often asked what I think of the toy train hobby and where I think it's going. When I offer my different views, whether in conversations at my store or in the pages of *Classic Toy Trains*, I take many factors into consideration.

On the supply side, I look at the new product lines and how customers are tending to receive them. Also important are the used trains entering the market in many different ways. On the demand side, I look at the folks young and old getting into the hobby. I see what the major manufacturers of toy trains are doing to create new business and inspire consumers about their efforts.

Let's start with the new folks that are getting into the hobby. According to an assortment of statistics, more than 10,000 people reach the age of 65 in this country every day! Age 65 is generally accepted as the normal retirement age. Once retired, people search for a hobby they believe can satisfactorily fill their remaining years. My experience tells me this point is true. Recently retired guys walk into my store and tell me they want to start collecting vintage O or S gauge trains. Or they want to build a layout with new models.

This promising trend should continue for at least 15 more years, based on population statistics and the number of older people. Now add in the steady flow of children who like toy trains. The retired folks I'm referring to are often grandparents willing to buy trains for youngsters.

What's behind the fascination little boys and girls have for toy trains? From what I hear at my store, we can thank two cultural icons: the books and videos featuring Thomas the Tank Engine and the children's book *The Polar Express*.

Smart of Lionel to develop an O gauge version of the steam engine and heavyweight passenger cars pictured in *The Polar Express*. I believe it has become the most popular train set of all time.

An important factor to be considered regarding the state of the hobby is the need for all major toy train manufacturers to advertise in the hobby media.

Prewar, postwar, and modern "pre-owned" trains are bought and sold in the marketplace every day via the Internet, public train shows, formal auctions, and in small stores like mine.

This market varies daily. It depends on who is buying and who is selling. Many collections are being sold, which affects the supply side. Used trains sell well, as long as the price is right and depending on their condition.

Many hobbyists are interested in new trains only. The latest products are superbly designed and are very attractive.

Still, manufacturers have priced them high, which dampens demand. I don't have many customers who can easily spend more than $1,000 for a new locomotive. Instead, there ought to be beautiful and reliable models for less than $300.

Luckily, manufacturers have taken steps to bring out reasonably priced starter sets. Now they need to follow up with additional accessories for children.

I see another good year. I look forward to spending many days working with the folks just getting into the hobby and the old-timers enjoying this great pastime.

Keep searchin'

PLASTICS—IN ONE WORD!

WHAT AN IMPACT PLASTICVILLE HAS HAD ON OUR HOBBY

FOR THOSE OF YOU WHO remember the 1967 movie *The Graduate* starring a very young Dustin Hoffman and the lovely Anne Bancroft, one line stands out. You may recall the older man giving advice to Hoffman, who played a recent college graduate. He offered a tip on future investments: "Just one word—plastics."

The toy train hobby discovered the importance of plastics approximately 20 years before that motion picture was released across America.

The late 1940s was when Bachmann Bros. started to make colorful miniature buildings made of injection-molded plastic. Those structures worked with O and S gauge trains. They also were used in the villages under many Christmas trees.

The assorted Plasticville buildings provided a "modern" look during the postwar era. No wonder kids loved them and spent their precious money on them.

My fondest memories of Christmas tree villages included the Plasticville buildings that would snap together. Those toy structures formed the fantasy world I would create with my American Flyer train under our family's Christmas tree. I also included a "lake" (really a mirror surrounded by artificial snow) with die-cast metal ice skaters. I think everybody had one of those lakes.

The Plasticville U.S.A. line featured many buildings to choose from, and they were all inexpensive. Houses, stores, municipal facilities, factories, railroad stations, and barns were just a few of the array.

They were even better with a string of white Christmas lights placed in each building. Everything seemed to come alive when light shined through the translucent walls of each structure. I loved all of them!

When I constructed my first O gauge layout at The Underground Railroad Shop in 1985, I knew Plasticville structures would be used everywhere. I had more than 200 buildings to thrill visitors to my store in New Castle, Pa., and leave them imagining they had gone back in time to the store displays of the 1950s.

In the 30 years since then, I have made many changes to the layout. I've even replaced of the Plasticville buildings with structures from the Snow Village line put out by Department 56. I've also kitbashed a number of unique items (most equipped with lights) to add realism to my layout.

Yet, I miss the clean look of the Plasticville buildings. I may add a section to the layout that includes only Plasticville items.

Meanwhile, my good friend Bill Nole, dubbed "The Mayor of Plasticville" for an article that appeared in the October 1992 issue of *Classic Toy Trains*, had the most complete Plasticville layout I have ever seen. You may recall that Bill had more than 500 Plasticville structures on his O gauge model railroad.

Plasticville remains one of the most collected areas of accessories in today's hobby. The Plasticville Collectors Organization (PCO) is made up of people who collect and promote the collection of Plasticville items. The group publishes a regular newsletter, *The Villager,* and in its pages you can learn about rare Plasticville items and interesting finds made by members.

A tribute should be paid to Bachmann for producing this wonderful line of miniature buildings and other accessories that fit well with our hobby and railroad villages. By the way, the best history of Plasticville I know of appeared in an article CTT Senior Editor Roger Carp wrote for the September 1998 issue of the magazine. Don't miss it.

Toy trains and Plasticville—a marriage made in hobby heaven!

Keep searchin'

"THE MOTHER OF ALL TRAIN SHOWS"

NOTHING IN THE WORLD OF TOY TRAINS BEATS YORK

CHRISTMAS COMES THREE TIMES A year for me—and many other toy train collectors and operators. Maybe you're one of them, or will someday join our ranks.

December 25 has always been my favorite traditional holiday. The joy I share with my extended family and friends during the holiday season has always been special.

The two other Christmases in my life come every April and October. These are the times when I attend toy train shows organized by the Eastern Division of the Train Collectors Association (TCA). The meets are held for a few days about the third week of every April and October, each year at the York Fairgrounds in York, Pa. Everybody refers to the train show as "York."

I've been going to York for more than 30 years. And, no, I have never—I mean never—missed a single show in all that time. That is how great York is!

When I first attended, the show opened on Friday morning and ended on Saturday afternoon. A few years ago, officers of the Eastern Division extended the show to three days, opening the halls at noon on Thursday.

For nearly all of its history, the meet has been held at the county fairgrounds. Early on, attendees needed three buildings to display what they intended to sell. Members walked through the aisles, gazing at Standard, O gauge, and S gauge from every era of toy train production. If you looked hard enough, you could spot European trains and cool memorabilia.

Members who arrived before the official show opened would open their car trunks and sell trains in the parking lots of hotels where they were staying. They even brought trains into the rooms, and guys would go from room to room looking at the beautiful trains displayed on the beds and tables of each room.

I remember finalizing good deals in those parking lots and rooms, whether early in the morning outdoors or late at night inside. The unofficial "bandit" meets were terrific ways to prepare for the official meet.

Not as much goes on in different parking lots and hotel rooms these days, especially after the show grew to three days. In the meantime, the York show has grown over the years until it now requires eight buildings for all the activity.

These days, more than 12,000 TCA members and their guests, including representatives from the major toy train manufacturers and publishers, make the semi-annual pilgrimage to what I call, "The Greatest Train Show On Earth."

More important than the trains bought and sold at York are the friendships developed among people with a common love of a great hobby. I can't begin to name all the friends I've made there—and the incredible trains I've seen and will probably never own.

Everyone seems to be happy at York. As I wrote in my book, *I Never Met a Train I Didn't Like*: "Toy train collectors are like a group of fifth graders on a scavenger hunt. If you notice the expression on the faces of the guys as they walk around a train show or first enter a train store, you'll see the excitement and anticipation of a great 'find.'"

So if you want the time of your life and have always dreamed of returning to fifth grade, be sure to attend York. Buy a train there, and make a new friend!

Keep searchin'

COWBOYS AND TRAINS
ELECTRIC TRAINS GO GREAT WITH
CERTAIN OTHER TOYS FROM POSTWAR DAYS

I RAN INTO A GOOD friend and passionate toy collector: Gene Scala. He once owned the largest collection in the world of Marx play sets. Each of those popular postwar toys consisted of a main structure, smaller buildings, and figures, all related to a theme, such as the Wild West.

In the late 1970s, Gene bought the entire inventory of play sets remaining at the Marx factory in Glendale, W.Va. He needed more than 30 trailers to ship the entire load to his home in New Castle, Pa.

I've known Gene for years and enjoy talking with him. Too bad I wasn't collecting toys when he owned the play sets.

During our recent visit I asked Gene about one of my favorite Marx play sets, one I had owned when I was young: the Roy Rogers Western Town play set.

The set contained a two-floor storefront of a Western town like folks saw in movies. Fashioned out of beautifully lithographed metal pieces, it featured the facades of structures typically found in a frontier community. They included a bank, a barbershop, a saloon, and a jail house. The interiors were finished with the back wall open, which made playing with them more fun.

Also packed inside the box were a ranch house, a stagecoach, fencing, and tepees and totem poles. There were lots of plastic cowboys, Indians, and horses, among the other "accessories" Marx designers added.

I enjoyed playing with my Roy Rogers Western Town while sitting on the floor of our living room in front of a black-and-white TV. I watched all the Western movies and shows aired on TV during the 1950s.

The first train layout at my train store featured the storefront from a Roy Rogers Western Town play set. I arranged it in a scene that included cowboys, horses, wagons, and other western figures.

There was a mountain nearby, and it had a tunnel for a Lionel General train set to run through before circling around the frontier scene. I added an Indian village, complete with tepees, campfires, and a river running through the village.

Western scenes are compatible with layouts. Luckily, figures of cowboys and Indians are easy to find. They blend nicely with a frontier town and railroad, along with the mountains, mesas, and deserts associated with the Old West.

Trains were major parts of American history—and not always in a good way. Westerns were highlighted by train robberies. In fact, the St. Louis Midland RR offered a $500 reward for the arrest of Jesse James.

Stop by my store these days and you won't see my original Western town. It gave way to a large amusement park. But I knew the layout needed a frontier scene. So I built an elevated platform complete with a Lionel Western backdrop.

As a teenager I built a model of a frontier fort. Known as Fort Apache, it had gun towers and a building inside with a stone chimney made from many pebbles glued together to form a realistic smokestack.

Well, you can still see that fort on my layout. Nearby, more than 100 cowboys, cavalry soldiers, and Indians are battling. A stagecoach and a covered wagon fill out the scene. A Lionel General chugs around it.

Cowboys and toy trains make any layout a complete picture of Americana. Consider adding an Old West scene to your railroad. Maybe you can put in structures and figures from a Marx Roy Rogers Western Town.

Keep searchin'

SELLER'S REMORSE
BETTER THINK TWICE BEFORE GETTING RID OF YOUR TOY TRAINS

I'M OFTEN ASKED BY CUSTOMERS and hobby friends, "When is a good time to sell my toy trains?" My standard reply is, "When you absolutely have to sell them."

What about me? To be honest with you, I hope I'll never have to sell my trains. I want to enjoy owning my vintage and current models as long as I can.

Thinking about this subject reminds me of a fellow I met a few years ago. We were chatting about the hobby. He had decided to sell some of his "extra" trains at a local train meet.

That guy could not believe the response. He told me the trains he was selling were only duplicates – items he had up-graded over the years and so had no use for. They had been piling up so he bought a table for the first time as a seller.

He priced the trains modestly in order to sell them, and he did, all of them!

Can you guess where the story is going? That guy enjoyed the experience so much that he decided to sell more of the trains he had collected at two other shows. I told him that he was turning into a train dealer. He laughed about that.

I was right. He now makes sure to buy multiple tables at the train shows put on by the Eastern Division of the Train Collectors Association in York, Pa. As a result he has sold nearly all of his collection.

The fellow liked the action as well as all the money he was raking in. Frankly, once you pull the plug on your collection it's hard to put on the brakes. The momentum builds, and you end up creating a selling frenzy.

The last time I saw that guy he reported that most of his trains were gone. Then he quickly confessed to feeling empty because he no longer owned some of the beautiful trains he had meticulously collected over the years. The money was nice, but he admitted to missing his trains and feeling sorry he had moved so fast.

Yes, we're talking about a severe case of what I call, "seller's remorse." I suggested he take some of the money and start to replace some of his favorite trains. He said he tried doing that and got "sticker shock" when he priced some of the same trains he had owned and recently sold for less money.

That's probably the reason why his trains sold so fast. Of course, he did make a profit. After all, he had bought them years ago at much lower prices.

That's it. The fellow now has a bag of money and empty shelves at home. I doubt he'll ever replace his trains and is more likely to become a train dealer than a train collector. He'll start to buy trains for the sole purpose of selling them. Good luck with that! He may be a little late to the party.

I became a dealer more than 30 years ago, when things were a lot different in the market. Given what I know, I wouldn't want to start today buying trains strictly for the purpose of selling them. The supply of trains has saturated the market, and there seems to be a fair market value equalizing costs versus profit.

I do not collect many trains now. I do have a nice collection and no room to fit more on my shelves. If I add something to my collection, I like to remove something and that's tough. I don't want to catch a bad case of seller's remorse.

Keep searchin'

OCTOBER

RAILROAD WARS
MEMORIES OF WHAT REAL TRAINS DID FOR MY FAMILY

I OFTEN LIKE TO INCLUDE stories about the actual railroads in my Views From The Underground columns. This makes perfect sense because, like so many of you, my lifelong love for toy trains stems from my lifelong love for the real thing.

Each time I work on the O gauge model railroad in my store or hold a collectible model in my hand, my mind slips back to the days when my dad worked on the Pennsylvania RR in our hometown of New Castle, Pa.

My parents came to America with their families at the turn of the 20th century. Many people living in our part of the Keystone State had emigrated from rural towns in southern Italy in the early 1900s.

In 1917, my father started to work at the car shop the Pennsy had erected in New Castle. He was only 17 years old, but said he was 19 to get the job. Heavy work was done at the car shop, including at a hot and dangerous foundry. Laborers melted steel to form parts for the mammoth trains that were being repaired.

One of Dad's early jobs was that of a burner, and our family has photos of him returning from work looking like a raccoon. Only his eyes were clean. The rest of his face was covered with smoke film from metal welding he performed.

The immigrants in our town worked hard, being glad to have jobs that enabled them to feed their families. They felt great loyalty for what they called "their" railroad.

Our town was split between folks who like Dad, worked for the Pennsy and other who were employed by the rival Baltimore & Ohio. Each group boasted about the superiority of their railroad. In fact, the rivalry was good natured, although sometimes the arguments would

121

get quite spirited and animated, especially when the guys were playing boccie at one of the local fraternal clubs.

The community grew around the railroads. Residents earned a good living and traveled thanks to free rail transportation. The railroads also sponsored summer picnics at Kennywood Amusement Park in Pittsburgh, as thousands of railroaders and their families came from all over western Pennsylvania to relax. Annual Christmas parties were other great social events for all employees.

Before the 1950s, the immigrant workers were never given the plum jobs, such as conductors and locomotive engineers. Later that changed. The railroads unionized, and promotions were made by seniority and the ability to do the job.

I've lived by railroads all of my life. I have many wonderful memories of visiting railroad yards, including the world's largest freight yard in Conway, Pa., which is about 30 miles south of New Castle. Visiting was a highlight of my younger days.

Who could ever forget the beautiful Pennsylvania RR calendar we would get every year? I loved to flip through them and look at the fantastic illustrations of Pennsy trains. Too bad my father never saved those classic calendars.

My frequent rail trips to Chicago and other cities were also special. I could write a book about my memories of the classic steam and diesel locomotives, the crack passenger trains, and, of course, the workers.

So you see my love for O and S gauge trains, whether vintage models or contemporary ones, always opens the door of my mind to many happy memories.

Keep searchin'

WHAT WE TAKE FOR GRANTED
IT'S TOO EASY TO OVERLOOK
WHAT MEANS THE MOST TO US

REMEMBER HOW I WROTE ABOUT my father? I forgot to mention his name! Frank Anthony Palumbo was the Pennsylvania railroader who gave me all the love of trains I have. For that, as I said in the column "Railroad Wars," I wanted to say, "Thanks, Dad." Too often, as I realized after omitting my dad's name, we take for granted the things and people that mean the most to us.

Our toy train collections include many beautiful and cherished sets. During the years we collect, we typically focus on the items we're searching. The hunt for these items is a lot of fun. Then, if we're lucky, we find them and add them to our stable of favorite trains. Do we pause to enjoy them? Or do we put them aside and move on to what we want next? Each of us has many trains that have been packed away for years. Too often we forget what we even own.

Well, just as I wanted to make sure you knew the name of my dad, I want to reflect on four of my favorite trains I have taken for granted. They are not the most valuable items in my collection or the scarcest. But these sets, which I confess I have taken for granted, stand at the heart of what I have.

Start with my American Flyer no. 5003T passenger set from 1950. This was my first set, and happy memories of playing with it when I was a boy rush back whenever I take it out. I have added a no. 654 heavyweight observation to the baggage car and two coaches that came with it. This would be the last set I'd ever sell—and I don't plan to sell any of my personal collection.

Second is my Lionel Congressional Limited passenger set from 1979. The streamlined train featured F3 A-B-A diesels on the point, with eight aluminum cars decorated for the Pennsylvania RR behind. I love this set because it features the Tuscan red F3s I waited each year for Lionel to produce during the postwar era. Sadly, it never did. This train has special meaning because my family would ride it from Pennsylvania to Chicago every summer in the 1950s. I'll always remember those diesels roaring past our station and braking so we could board.

Next is the Lionel no. 2140WS outfit from 1948. A no. 671 turbine and tender came with three no. 2400-series coaches painted green with gray roofs. I wanted this great set from the moment I first saw it in the 1948 catalog, mostly because of the mammoth Pennsy 6-8-6 locomotive. I have since acquired a fantastic example and then added two more coaches to create a train I see as really remarkable. To be honest, I own many more Lionel steam sets that are worth more, but none that I appreciate more. Yet my pristine 2140WS is a set I hate to say I have occasionally taken for granted.

Fourth on my list is my American Flyer no. 5002T circus train from 1950. I own all of the top Flyer freight and passenger sets, but this one remains my favorite. As collectors know, the circus set came with a no. 353 die-cast metal steamer painted red, plus a bright yellow coach and two yellow flatcars, each of which carried two colorful cages and a tractor-trailer. I have added four flatcars with loads and two coaches to form an impressive train. It reflects my lifelong love of circuses and carnivals as well as my boyhood wish to run away to live and work under the Big Top.

So there you have it! The four vintage train sets I often take for granted. What are the most overlooked trains among your favorite sets? Let us know by dropping a note or sending an email to CTT. We'll share what we learn from you.

Keep searchin'

THE MAGIC OF THE CIRCLE
A MOVING TRAIN DELIGHTS EVERY ONE OF US

WHAT IS IT THAT MESMERIZES—just hypnotizes—each of us whenever we can watch a model train travel around a circle? Whether we are young, middle-aged, or somewhat past our prime, we can't resist looking at a train set as it moves.

How many of you would agree that, since we were children in the postwar era, we have never passed by any opportunity to watch trains go around the track through the tiny villages under a Christmas tree or on a display?

Speaking for myself, I really miss the evenings back in the 1950s when my family would go downtown to visit the stores at Christmas time.

The shops were open until 9 o'clock on Monday and Thursday evenings throughout the holiday season, starting right after Thanksgiving. That's when it was the most fun to see all the decorations and holiday lights put up in town.

My parents, siblings, and I would walk from store to store to admire their window displays. Every store had a eye-catching display in its window. And nearly all of those displays included a miniature electric train set or two traveling through a village made up of commercial or handmade structures.

I always liked the scene in the movie, The Godfather, showing Michael and Kay Corleone as they shopped at night in New York City. They were looking through a store window with a Lionel train going around a toy village.

Those type of scenes—slices of Americana—were added to many movies. They reflected the evenings I remember from growing up in typical town while shopping with my family as the holidays approached.

125

Kids and grown-ups stood in front of store windows, looking as though they were in a wonderful trance. Nothing can match those evenings and the folks walking through the snow carrying their packages during this holiday season. I love those days and think about them every time I see a model train chugging around the track of a layout, no matter how small and simple it is.

When I was a boy I spent many hours during the Christmas season laying my head sideways on the living room floor, watching my American Flyer train as it ran around our Christmas tree village. I would put my head on the floor in right front of the tunnel and watch the oncoming train headlight as it passed through the tunnel with lighted passenger cars following. How many of you did that too?

Many times I would fall asleep as I dreamed of the places that train was going. You've never lived until you put your head on the carpet by a layout. I see the same magic today in my store when people stop in to watch the different trains going around our O gauge layout. I purposely did not include any switch track on it because I didn't want to increase chances for derailment.

No one likes to have a train derail while enjoying the magic of a lighted city with trains traveling around and through it. So I included dog-bone loops and different levels of action to add animation and excitement. Trains run over 14 circles of track.

Children and adults stand in one spot watching each train go around the circles of track while they are daydreaming of many wonderful times. The magic of the circle has touched millions of kids of all ages. Every holiday season this magic returns. I hope it will continue until the end of time.

Our hobby increases this magic. Please do everything you can to preserve the beauty and thrills of toy trains, passing the magic to future generations.

Merry Christmas and Happy Holidays!

PART 2:
I Still Haven't Met a Train I Didn't Like

ESSAYS FROM 2016

A LESSON TO BE LEARNED
PART ONE: EVERYTHING BEGAN WITH THE BUY

I HAVE BOUGHT AND SOLD many toy trains since opening my store, the Underground Railroad Shoppe, in New Castle, Pa., in 1985. More than I can count! Trains from every manufacturer and era.

A lot of the trains I buy and sell are mint sets and locomotives from recent decades. But most come from the prewar and postwar eras. I'm talking about American Flyer, Lionel, and Marx. I never know what someone will offer me. That's one of the fun parts of owning a store. I love looking through the boxes of old trains people bring into the store for sale. I also enjoy making visits to homes to buy larger collections.

Believe me, I could relate dozens of stories about the train deals I have made over the past 35 years. There are enough to write a book…maybe I will.

Now, however, I'd like to share one of the buying experiences I have had. Maybe it will serve as a lesson to anyone buying and selling used trains today. One day, while I was working behind the counter in my store, two young fellows walked in. They were carrying some cardboard boxes filled with used Lionel trains. I didn't get too excited. No big deal. It's is a common occurrence.

Usually when I buy trains from strangers I ask where the trains are from and who owns them. The two guys told me while cleaning out their grandfather's house they had discovered them in the attic and were given the trains. The boxes were very dusty. They contained postwar and prewar trains in average condition.

After examining the trains I made what I considered a fair offer for the entire lot. I offered the two guys $400. Without any hesitation, they accepted it.

I always buy toy trains with a company check and I ask for some form of identification from the seller. I made the check to the fellow who showed his ID.

Over the years I can recall times when people selling trains insisted on being paid in cash only. That leaves me suspicious about the trains' ownership. I pass on buying trains from people who won't accept a check or refuse to show an ID. I do so to protect my business from buying trains that may be stolen.

Going back to the story...a week or two after paying the two guys a man and a woman walked into my store with a police officer. The couple had been there earlier and spotted some trains that were familiar to them.

The two people stated that a few of the trains I displayed on shelves looked like trains that had been stolen from their father's home, which had been vacant since he died a year ago.

I told the officer I had purchased the trains with a check and been shown an identification card by one of the sellers.

The officer requested that I turn over the trains to him so they could be used as evidence of a crime. He stated that when the fellows were found a hearing would take place and the magistrate would notify me. I packed up the trains and handed them over to the police officer. At that point, I did not have the trains or the money I had paid for them.

Buying used toy trains usually is generally a positive experience because most of the people selling them—heirs, collectors, and or original owners—obtained them the right way. When the trains come to me dishonestly, I feel bad.

What happened after the police officer took the trains? I'll conclude my story, which had a surprising ending, in the next issue of *Classic Toy Trains*.

Keep searchin'

A LESSON TO BE LEARNED
PART TWO: EVERYTHING ENDED WITH THE HEARING

IN THE JANUARY ISSUE OF *Classic Toy Trains*, I wrote about how I had once bought a group of Lionel trains at my store I subsequently learned might have been stolen. In this column, I will finish telling the story and add what I learned and how it might help all of you.

We can resume with my being contacted by one of the police officers who had confiscated the toy trains from my store that were alleged to have been stolen. He called to inform me that the two suspected thieves had been apprehended.

The officer said a hearing had been scheduled at which I would be expected to testify. It was going to be held at the office of the district magistrate, with a judge in attendance to preside over the hearing.

Naturally, I appeared on the selected day to testify regarding what I knew about the facts behind the case.

When I arrived I saw the couple that had come to my store and identified the trains. I also noticed the officer who had confiscated the trains, all of them placed on a table in the front of the courtroom.

Finally, I spied the two fellows who had sold me the trains. One of them, accompanied by another officer, was dressed in an orange prisoner jumpsuit.

The hearing began with my testimony reflecting the events surrounding my purchase of the trains. The judge asked me if I could state with certainty those were the trains taken from the complainants.

I answered that, unless the trains had specific identifying marks, there was no way to state with assurance they were the ones supposedly taken from their father's home. All I could say with certainty was the confiscated trains were the very same ones I had purchased from the suspects.

Meanwhile, the suspects had changed their story about how they had acquired the toy trains. They now claimed they had found them in a dumpster. They said they had told me the story of finding them while cleaning their grandfather's attic for fear I would not buy trains that were found in a dumpster.

The judge dismissed the case against the suspects because the police could not prove the two had taken the trains from the home. Also, without specific marks on the trains, they couldn't prove they were the trains allegedly stolen.

Needless to say, the couple disagreed with the ruling. They wanted to take the trains even though no charges had been placed against the two suspects. But the judge awarded the trains to me because I had shown proof of purchase. I offered them to the people for what I had paid. They refused.

What can all of us learn from this experience? Simple—mark every toy train in your collection in some way in order to show proof of ownership.

An easy method is to put address stickers on the inside of the shells of engines and different pieces of rolling stock.

Another good idea is to stamp your name on the bottom of your trains using invisible ink seen only with a black light. This inexpensive method works well and doesn't compromise the value of trains.

Taking photo of all your toy trains does not provide adequate proof of ownership because many collectible trains look alike. Buy sufficient insurance to replace trains in the event of theft, flood, or fire.

I have followed these recommendations because of what took place in my store and at the district magistrate's office years ago. I hope my story gives you something to consider doing to protect your trains.

Keep searchin'

DINERS, DRIVE-INS & TRAINS
TOY TRAIN MAKERS FEED OUR APPETITE FOR DINERS

EVERYONE WHO KNOWS ME KNOWS that I like to cook and to eat. I worked in the kitchen at a hospital during my high school and college years. I learned to cook there and still love to cook.

I like to watch the Food Channel on television, and one of my favorite shows is Diners, Drive-Ins and Dives, featuring Guy Fieri. He does a swell job visiting diners and similar restaurants all over the country. I like to see the styles of the diners Guy visits and the unique dishes they serve.

Watching those shows got me thinking about how much diners have long been part of the railroad scene—on full-size and miniature railroads.

Many of the first diners were made from old Pullman cars their owners had remodeled into restaurants. They popped up all over America during the late 1930s and '40s. Think of all scenes in old movies that included diners.

It didn't take long for toy manufacturers to produce diners as accessories for their model trains. Even before the prewar era came to an end, Lionel was cataloging its no. 442 diner. Like the real thing, that diner started life as a tinplate passenger car. Lionel always knew what it was doing.

My first diner—and still my favorite—was the no. 767 Branford diner made by the A.C. Gilbert Co. for its S gauge line of American Flyer trains. I loved the nostalgic artwork added to the yellow heavyweight Pullman car. Remember? It promised "Good Eats" on the roof sign. The roof also has a red chimney and kind of primitive metal television antenna so many of us had on our houses.

The signage on the front of the Branford diner read, "Booths for Ladies" and "Television Every Nite." Steaks and chops were also advertised on the front of the diner. The plastic diner was illuminated and mounted on a green metal base. The 767 fed my interest in diners, and I have been collecting them ever since. Visit the O gauge layout in my store, and you will see plenty of them.

Another favorite, also part of the Flyer line, was the no. 275 Eureka diner. After getting one of those, I wanted one of the diners in the Plasticville line in the 1950s. I began to add as many diners as I could on the layout. Now I have 10. I'm always looking for more to install.

Luckily, the list of diners and drive-ins for toy trains keeps growing. I think of Shelly's Diner and Dinah's Drive-In from Department 56. Of course, there are the Lionelville Diner and the new Luxury Diner (also a Lionel product). Williams released the Madison Diner, which, like the old Branford diner, consists of a Pullman car secured to a flat base.

The best-looking diner was produced by K-Line a few years back, and I added it to my layout this year. The Starlite Diner was made from a shiny streamlined coach complete with many lights and a detailed lighted interior placed on a composition base complete with paved parking spaces.

What else? How about Frankie's Hot Dog Shop and Krispy Kreme Donut Shop from Department 56? MTH Electric Trains gave us Mel's Diner. And you can find models of a McDonald's drive-in and a White Castle restaurant, too.

Yep, I love diners and drive-ins with my toy trains. They go together like a burger and fries and give a great feeling of nostalgia to any O or S gauge layout.

There's nothing like seeing an old steamer coupled to a passenger train passing a warmly lit diner in one of the small towns filling our fantasy train world. Maybe it's time you added a vintage or new diner to your home layout.

Keep searchin'

THE FACE OF TOY TRAIN BUYERS—THEN AND NOW
THE CHANGING IDENTITY OF TYPICAL HOBBYISTS

EVER GIVEN MUCH THOUGHT TO who is buying electric trains? As the owner of a store selling new and vintage trains, I need to pay close attention to who my customers are. I continue to learn about them, and so I wanted to share some of my impressions.

I opened the Underground Railroad Shoppe in 1985. Over the past three decades, I've seen the face of the train buyer change a lot. Six years prior to opening the store, I had been buying used trains and selling them at train shows all over the country. My store became an extension of the shows I had been attending. As a result, I relied on the vintage trains I had found for most of my initial inventory.

I rented tables and placed them in front of the aluminum shelves installed on the walls of the showroom. I displayed the trains on the tables and shelves. Nearly all the trains I offered at first were vintage models, along with used track and switches of all gauges. Quickly, though, I was supplementing the older trains and accessories with new items purchased from Lionel as well as wholesale distributors. Looking back, most of that new inventory amounted to starter sets, accessories, and track.

Within a year or two, I had replaced those tables with illuminated display cases. I was transforming my little shop into a regular retail sales store, featuring a full line of trains and all the items that complement them. Specifically, I stocked light bulbs, landscaping materials, structures, and figures needed for layouts.

The main customer base of my store back in the 1980s and '90s consisted primarily of men between the age of 35 and 55. Baby boomers—to put it plainly—who were searching for Lionel and American Flyer trains from the postwar period—the trains they had enjoyed in their youth.

During the holiday season, I saw high sales of new Lionel starter sets (priced between $80 and $100). They typically had an all-plastic locomotive and a few cars.

At the same time, I was going through my inventory of O gauge diecast metal steam engines equipped with smoke and a whistle as well as the dozens of commonplace freight cars. My staff and I put together sets with the used items, along with track and small transformers, on hand.

Our newly created postwar train sets were seen as more desirable than the cheesy sets being made by Lionel. To our satisfaction, the starter sets later developed by Lionel and MTH rapidly improved in quality.

Kids were not as involved as their dads in the early years. Meanwhile, Lionel was producing superior trains for adult collectors. Many of my customers began collecting the new trains.

The shifting interests of the people stopping by caused me to transform my store and the inventory being stocked. Soon, we were filling the shelves with new collectibles. Meanwhile, the quantities of older trains displayed were diminishing, mainly because the numbers available for me to purchase continued to decline.

The final decade of the 20th century ushered in the era I generally refer to "Train Wars." Challenging Lionel for dominance on the current market were K-Line, MTH, and Williams. Competition for toy train dollars was heating up!

Join me in the next issue of *Classic Toy Trains*, when I'll explore Train Wars and bring the tale up to date. We'll see the face of the train buyer of today!

Keep searchin'

"TRAIN WARS"

HOW THE FACE OF THE TYPICAL HOBBYIST HAS EVOLVED

IN THE MAY ISSUE OF *Classic Toy Trains*, I launched my discussion of who has been buying toy trains since I opened the Underground Railroad Shoppe in 1985. You might recall how I focused on what was going in the final years of the 20th century, with an emphasis on events in the 1990s I referred to as "Train Wars."

I remember the 1990s as a time when lots of new blood entered our hobby. The cause and effect of that significant change was the great increase in the availability of new toy trains.

Lionel had been the main supplier of all new O gauge trains during the 1970s and '80s. K-Line and Williams were beginning to produce trains, but they did not then offer much competition to Lionel.

Around that time the person who, in my opinion, has done more for O gauge trains than any other in recent memory entered the hobby: Mike Wolf, who established and still leads MTH Electric Trains.

Under Mike's leadership, MTH began to produce high-quality trains at competitive prices. And it introduced ProtoSound, which was the best sound system.

Other manufactures had to improve their lines to compete with MTH Electric Trains. Fortunately for us, they did!

Lionel rose to the challenge, improving the quality and expanding the variety of its trains. K-Line and Williams followed suit. They made more and better trains.

The train market went crazy during the 1990s. The economy was excellent during those "Clinton-Dot Com" years. People were spending money like they were mad at it! How do I know? Frankly, the 1990s represented the most profitable years I've ever had at my store.

Good times continued into the 21st century. The introduction by Lionel of models inspired by Thomas the Tank Engine and Friends brought into the hobby children who might otherwise not have been enticed by O gauge modeling.

Lionel took another major step forward when it brought out the Polar Express train set in 2005. That event encouraged more children to enjoy trains. Why, the Polar Express became the largest selling O gauge set of all time!

Today, many of the recently retired guys who were not buying trains in the past 30 years, are getting into the hobby. They have an interest in operating trains and building a layout at home rather than collecting vintage models.

Many of these baby boomers tell their wives, "Grandpa is building a layout for the grandkids to enjoy." Grandma gives immediate approval to such an expenditure. She might even join in all the good times.

At the same time, I still see newlyweds in my store who are buying their first set. They have in mind entertaining their yet-to-arrive or newly born children with a train around the Christmas tree.

Baby boomers and newlyweds—everyone having the shared goal of helping boys and girls enjoy toy trains. I really believe more children are involved in the O gauge hobby now than was the case back in the 1980s and '90s.

Which is fantastic! I think the train hobby will always exist. To use an old cliché, it is as American as apple pie. Trains were part of everyone's youth, and a toy train always generates warm feelings of family, home, and nostalgia when it is part of an imaginary village layout or arranged to run under a Christmas tree.

The past 40 years made history in the hobby: new companies, innovative technologies, books and videos, and strong train collecting clubs. I'm glad I witnessed the growth and look ahead to much more!

Keep searchin'

AN APPRECIATION OF MIKE WOLF
NO ONE HAS RECENTLY DONE MORE
TO PROMOTE O GAUGE

CONVERSATION AND NOT CONTROVERSY IS my goal when writing for *Classic Toy Trains*. I like to spark people to think about what is going on rather than start arguments. Well, I did a little of both in a recent column.

When looking at how the O gauge side of the hobby has developed since 1990, I made a clear and bold statement. I wrote that the person who has done the most to promote O gauge modeling over the past 25 years is Mike Wolf, founder and president of MTH Electric Trains.

I first met Mike way back in 1983. We were among the dealers selling old trains at the Billy Budd Hotel in York, Pa. Longtime collectors remember the Billy Budd and all the buying and selling that went on before the start of the show sponsored by the Eastern Division of the Train Collectors Association.

My spot was next to Mike's in a field adjacent to the hotel. He was selling parts for prewar trains—not original components but reproductions manufactured by Williams. And the demand for those parts was huge; guys were thrilled to find new and reasonably priced items that fit on their antique trains.

Mike and the people working alongside him were so busy they could hardly keep up with the buyers. Here was a 23-year-old guy who plainly loved vintage trains and was a smart businessman. Mike had bought all the parts plus the dies to make more from his former boss and good friend, Jerry Williams.

Besides producing parts and avidly selling them, Mike spent time talking with other dealers and customers to learn what was needed in the hobby.

Mike's ability to listen and plan would pay off well. Even before leaving Williams, Mike had made connections with Samhongsa, a manufacturing company in Korea. Before long, it was making new versions of classic prewar locomotives and railcars for Mike to sell under the name Mike's Train House.

Mike soon took another important step and formed a relationship with Lionel Trains Inc. The contract negotiated with LTI called for him to make reissues of prewar trains and accessories for Lionel to market under its name. While that relationship did not last long, Mike moved ahead in the production of toy trains. Besides Standard gauge items, he expanded into O gauge. Not bringing back prewar items but creating great models of contemporary trains.

Luckily for Mike, he brought firsthand knowledge picked up from selling parts and then collaborating with Samhongsa on new trains.

Many corporations lack such firsthand experience in their top-level management positions. They rely on corporate "suits," consultants, and "bean counters" to give them accurate projections on what to introduce and how much to make. They depend on outsiders, not insiders.

This corporate mentality seldom has the experience needed to evaluate a market. Mike was able to apply his knowledge to MTH, which in 1994 changed the O gauge hobby forever with four innovations: ProtoSound, fan-driven smoke units, solid three-rail track with plastic roadbed, and the no. Z-4000 transformer. Those products raised the bar for competing businesses. K-Line, Lionel, and Williams soon developed similar   O gauge products. The same thing happened when MTH put on the market articulated steam locomotives.

Consumers enjoyed a much better selection of O gauge trains with additional features thanks to Mike Wolf. But, as I will explain next time, Mike was only beginning to reshape the toy train hobby.

Keep searchin'

MORE ABOUT MIKE WOLF
HOW THIS ENTREPRENEUR AND HOBBYIST
KEEPS CHANGING O GAUGE TRAINS

IN THE SEPTEMBER ISSUE OF *Classic Toy Trains*, I started describing how Mike Wolf, the founder and now president and CEO of MTH Electric Trains, has shaped the contemporary O gauge hobby. His impact has been so significant.

While working with Lionel in the late 1980s, Mike offered his help in making the Reading T1 steam engine. The partnership seemed ideal. With the help of Samhongsa manufacturing in Korea, Mike was able to arrange the production of several locomotives for Lionel while he was under contract with them.

However, there were disagreements between Mike and Lionel about the size of production runs. As a result, some collector engines and sets, including the reissues of the prewar Hiawatha outfit and the Rail Chief passenger cars, were produced in greater numbers than Mike recommended. Eventually, Mike and Lionel came to a parting of the ways.

Here's another case where Mike affected the hobby in a good way. A few years ago, the Union Pacific RR, concerned that model manufacturers were using its trademarks without permission, sought to impose a licensing fee. Licensing arrangements are common in the hobby industry. A maker of plastic automobile kits will negotiate a license deal with the car company—along with a separate deal for the right to reproduce the tire company's name on the sidewalls!

Mike had other ideas. He challenged the UP's plans. He noted there had been no objection in the many years toy trains had been carrying the name of full-size railroads. In fact, he said, there was a time railroads paid toy firms to use their names.

Mike won the argument. The UP agreed to drop its licensing proposal, a reversal that benefited all toy train manufacturers. It also benefited consumers, who were spared a price increase covering the cost of the licensing.

Mike has recently broadened the MTH line. His company now manufactures HO scale trains, along with O and Standard gauge trains. Mike has applied the innovations his firm pioneered to HO models. At the same time, Mike has expanded the range of O gauge products he is making. MTH now produces models of European locomotives and trains.

Mike believes the future of the toy train hobby is very bright. He has seen many children starting to run O and S gauge trains. Meanwhile, he notes, numbers of newly retired baby boomers are getting into the train hobby. Mike points out with satisfaction the World's Greatest Train Shows attract more than 30,000 people to each show. These crowds consist mostly of families, who are visiting displays by dealers and vendors.

He and I have had fun on the golf course. He never gets tired of telling a story about former Major League Baseball star Jose Canseco at the Dan Marino Celebrity Pro-Am Golf Tournament.

I had made a long putt for Mike's team, and Canseco, who had been in the group behind us, met us on the next tee and wanted to know who made that long putt on the previous hole. I proudly introduced myself to Canseco and claimed the honor of that putt. I proceeded to hit my tee shot and hooked my drive out of bounds. Jose yelled, "Lou, you better stick to putting!" All of us laughed at that.

Everything Mike Wolf and MTH have accomplished has encouraged all the other toy train manufacturers to compete and improve their different products. We've gained a lot—another reason I'm glad Mike was there.

Keep searchin'

THEY'RE TOYS AND NOT MUSEUM PIECES

AS OWNER OF THE UNDERGROUND Railroad Shoppe, I often have opportunities to purchase prewar and postwar electric trains. And I love it when they are in pristine condition. Sometimes people bring them to my store; occasionally I see them when I visit the home of whoever calls and wants to sell those beauties.

After marveling at how great those vintage locomotives and cars look, my mind starts to wonder about them. Specifically, why are they in like-new condition in their original boxes?

It seems those vintage electric trains were either never used or hardly ever put on O or S gauge track to run. I figure long ago children seldom got a chance to enjoy them.

Sometimes when I ask about the trains, the people selling them say, "Dad would set them up, and we were not allowed to touch them." Sad to hear.

Better is hearing the other kind of story. That happens when folks bring in well-used trains. I listen as they recall the fun they had when they were young.

The other day a fellow came into the store to share stories about the trains he had while growing up in the 1950s.

Fred Capotosto visited, and we had a great time as he looked around and swapped tales about the trains he had as a boy in my home state of Pennsylvania. By the way, his last name translates from Italian to English as "hard head." Fred insisted he wasn't, but his wife disagreed. Naturally, we all had a good laugh.

Fred still has an O gauge layout. He runs his dad's prewar trains as well as the Lionel trains and accessories he received from his parents during the 1950s. Soon, he was telling the story of the no. 726 RR Berkshire his sister and he raced long ago only to watch it fly off their train table. They bent the corner of the roof of the cab, but the steamer was otherwise fine.

Every time Fred sees the dent now, he fondly remembers his sister and the fun they had when they were really young.

Another story Fred told concerned a Lionel Lehigh Valley hopper. He drilled half a dozen small holes into one side. You see, after watching the 1964 movie Von Ryan's Express, Fred wanted to re-create a scene on his layout complete with "bullet holes." He recalled his dad being a little mad but mostly surprised when a young Fred had explained why he added the holes.

I can see the magic of toy trains as Fred reminisced about his adventures with Lionel engines and cars in the 1950s and '60s. He believed, as his father had said, they should be played with and not treated like museum pieces.

Trains have become a tradition in many households. They connect good feelings today to the assorted memories stirred up when we see or run them.

I still go crazy when I see vintage locomotives and railcars that have lasted in immaculate condition since being manufactured and brought home. Of course, to own them is a pleasure. It is how many of us built up big collections.

The rush I always get when I see one of those pristine prewar or postwar items has never changed. It is like something we can never get enough. To own such an item is what many collectors want. Those trains are truly museum pieces.

Yet when I see trains that were played with, I'm glad to see the enjoyment they must have brought to the children that own them. No wonder old trains bring back memories of family and the holiday season, when everything is at its best.

Keep searchin'

MEMORIES OF SONNY BOY, THE TRAIN STORE DOG

ON DECEMBER 26—THE DAY after Christmas—2004, I brought home a two-month-old Yellow Labrador Retriever. I named my brand-new puppy Sonny, after Sonny Corleone, a character in my all-time favorite movie, The Godfather.

Before long, I was bringing Sonny with me to my store every day. He immediately became a hit there.

Everyone made a fuss over this cute little puppy as he went through all of his growing pains at the store. Sonny soon established one "station" behind the main counter and another in my private office toward the rear of the store.

When Sonny got older, he had his own kennel in my office where he loved to stay. Not always, though.

Sonny would come out to greet customers on request. He gave them his paw to shake. I liked to think Sonny was encouraging them to buy trains from me. He was a great salesman.

Sonny loved to be at the store and seemed to know when I was leaving to go there each day the store was open. He would meet me at the front door of my house with his leash in his mouth.

When Sonny was younger, he crawled under the store layout where I was working. He would lay down beside me while I was doing some wiring or repairs. But as Sonny grew, I could not let him wander there. His big tail would tear wires out.

All Sonny could do then was wait outside of the layout when I worked beneath it. Even so, he was great company during the many hours I was working.

Sonny Boy loved to eat with the crew during the holidays. I didn't feed him people food, but he was always nearby to bum a French fry from one of the guys.

Everyone who came into the store knew Sonny and would ask to see him. On any of those rare occasions when Sonny missed a day at the store, I would always tell customers that he was off that day. People got a kick out of that.

Sonny loved the trains and would watch the trains in my lower layout as they traveled around. He would turn his head when he would hear the whistle. For some reason, he was never startled by any of the louder locomotive sounds.

The years rolled by too fast, and Sonny slowed down. He slept more in his kennel when he was at the office and started to develop breathing problems. Then it became part of my routine to give Sonny his medicine.

One day when Sonny was almost 12 years old, he started to breathe really heavy at the store. Worried about what was happening, I rushed him to our vet. The vet told us Sonny's lung problems had become serious, and she could not fix them. I had to have my pal put to sleep.

I never thought I would have felt such a loss. As I told my family and staff, there would never be another Sonny Boy. That feeling of loss lasted two weeks. I was missing my old friend so much I needed a dog. After trying to locate a rescue lab, I heard about an eight-week-old Black Labrador Retriever. I named him Dodger after my favorite baseball team.

Right now, Dodger is a real handful. He's just a puppy, right? But he is already working at the train store. Too bad everything there is a chew toy to him.

I love Dodger, but memories of Sonny will always last with me and all the people who come looking for him at the store.

Come in some time and get to know Dodger while remembering Sonny Boy.

Keep searchin'

PART 2:
I Still Haven't Met a Train I Didn't Like

ESSAYS FROM 2017

IT TAKES A VILLAGE
MORE MEMORIES OF POSTWAR CHRISTMAS CELEBRATIONS

SOME OF MY FIRST MEMORIES include celebrating Christmas at home. I was 4 or 5 years old—around 1948 or '49, that is—when I first remember the Christmas tree erected in the living room of our family home.

My mom and three older sisters were in charge of decorating the tree. I was assigned to watch and "not touch anything." The bulbs on the tree were very delicate and would break if they fell down or were knocked off.

My mother or one of my sisters placed a clean white sheet under the tree. Its purpose? A white sheet should represent a winter scene.

Then we set up a traditional manger scene on one side. There was an old looking wood stable with a manger, where the baby Jesus was placed with Mary and Joseph on each side. The figures were made of a chalk-like material that was brightly painted. They were fairly large figures, which today I would call G scale.

My family didn't stop there. The manger scene included almost 20 other ceramic figures. There were kind and loving shepherds as well as the three wise men mentioned in the Bible. Miniature angels and animals completed the scene.

Once my family had set up this scene, I was quickly instructed not to touch it either. I'm sure one of my sisters told me it represented the "holy part" of Christmas. After all, we were celebrating the birthday of Jesus during that season.

The rest of the bottom of the tree was filled with the Christmas village. There originally were no electric trains or any train-related items. I had yet to receive my very first American Flyer train set.

No problem! You see, I loved to play with that village. It included 15 to 20 houses made of a pretty solid material mostly white covered with

149

sparkling snow. Each one had a hole in the back wall for a Christmas light to illuminate through the cellophane red and yellow windows. They were stamped "Japan" on the underside of the base. We put a string of small Christmas lights in each house.

Over the years I have collected those houses because they remind me of my earliest Christmas village. I have always dreamed of creating a larger and more elaborate version of those villages. I look forward to doing that some day.

Looking back more than 65 years, I recall how my sisters and I added rolls of cotton near the houses. The cotton served as hills where we placed tiny skiers. We placed a round mirror on the sheet to serve as a lake. Then we sprinkled fake grass around the outline of the lake before adding a handful of miniature skaters.

We had a nice selection of metal figures by Barclay and Manoil. Besides skiers and sled riders, we had farm figures and animals. I still collect these sorts of figures today. They left a lasting impression that I still remember now.

Mom enhanced the scene with her illuminated model of a church. She kept it in her room, but always let us put it on the Christmas village to enjoy. We also had lots of die-cast metal figures to serve as carolers around the church.

A folded type of wood fence surrounded the entire village. It designated the point where imagination would take over and escort me into the wonderful fantasy that I had spent hours enjoying every holiday season. Nothing could beat lying on the floor and playing with the village on those cold winter nights

Nothing topped that experience until the wonderful Christmas when I got my first electric train. Then trains became an important part of that annual fantasy.

Best wishes to all of you: Merry Christmas and Happy Holidays.

DOWNSIZING

LEAVING THE HOBBY? EASIER SAID THAN DONE!

I RECEIVED AN ALL-TOO-familiar phone call recently while working at my train store. The fellow on the line said he and his wife were downsizing. They were planning to move into a smaller home in the near future. I knew immediately why he had me on the phone.

The guy had a "large O gauge layout." How large? He said it was 24x50 feet with multiple levels. There were more than 200 Dickens Village ceramic buildings from the Department 56 line, along with "hundreds" of figures.

Hearing his description, I assumed the layout must have many trains and accessories included with it. Surprisingly, that was not the case. The guy informed me he had only one track around the entire village that a train passed through.

Nearing the end of what the caller had to say, he told me the layout was still up. He wanted someone to buy it and then disassemble and remove it from his home. He would even toss in all the original boxes.

Now it was my turn to talk—and what I had to say wasn't about to please the fellow. I felt sorry for him because it was up to me to break the sad news about the hobby. To be blunt, his collection was not worth anything near what he paid for the items or what he thought it was worth.

In addition, I said, there would be a lot of work involved in dissembling the layout. More time-consuming might be the process of dusting and cleaning each one of the ceramic buildings before putting them in their original boxes.

The last I checked online, items from the Dickens Village line were selling at about 10 to 20 percent of their original retail price. To make matters worse, those already puny values depended on items still being like new in the box.

Then I did the math in my head. If the labor costs were deducted from the sale of the items, he would be lucky to get 10 cents on a dollar for his collection. Of course, I was offering my opinion only. But I was firm about one thing. There were not enough trains to justify buying his collection of ceramic structures.

This, needless to say, was only one of the many phone calls I receive from people who are downsizing. The scenario they describe is usually identical to this. But I have learned something about people eager to downsize and move into smaller homes, apartments, or condos. A friend I visited in Florida strikes me as typical. When he sold his home in Pennsylvania a few years ago, he liquidated his sizable collection of O gauge trains as well as a large and beautifully landscaped three-rail layout.

Anyway, when I stopped in at his new home, wouldn't you know a brand-new layout occupied a small bedroom. N scale! He is having a ball with it.

Should you plan to downsize and sell your trains, start by making a complete and detailed inventory. Then determine the value of what you have by consulting the latest Greenberg's Pocket Price Guides and Internet auction websites.

Doing your homework will help you avoid sticker shock when you sell your trains. Don't forget to add in the labor costs of packing and transportation.

Back to the fellow with the Department 56 layout. He did sell it all. But like my friend, he never got away from the toy train hobby. Instead, he and his wife now collect structures from a different part of the Department 56 line—Snow Village—they are proudly displaying in the dining room of their new condo.

Funny how the urge to collect is so gratifying it never leaves us. As I always say, "It's the hunt and not the kill that drives collecting in any hobby."

Keep searchin'

MARCH

BY POPULAR DEMAND
NOW EVERYONE CAN GO TO "YORK"

TOY TRAIN SHOWS HAVE BEEN critical to the development of this hobby. They're all fantastic, but one has dominated the field. I praised it in the May 2015 issue of *Classic Toy Trains* as "The Mother of All Train Shows."

"The Greatest Train Show on Earth" is organized by the Eastern Division of the Train Collectors Association (TCA) twice a year over three days, typically during the third week of April and October at the county fairgrounds in York, Pa. More than 11,000 TCA members usually attend each show, known as "York." What do attendees discover? More than seven buildings, or halls, filled with vintage and new trains and accessories available for sale. There are two dealer halls and four member halls and at least one building reserved for setting up modular layouts for viewing.

Members put out for sale thousands of trains. Individuals as well as retailers and even the best-known manufacturers bring their finest locomotives, cars, and more. The majority of items being sold are O gauge. But don't imagine the other sizes are ignored. Prewar, postwar, and modern-era trains ranging from Standard down to S and even OO and HO scale are represented. TCA members can even discover hard-to-find trains from England, France, Germany, and elsewhere.

The York experience has been open only to TCA members and their guests (permitted to attend just once). After going once, guests who wanted to return to York were required to join the TCA.

Times change, as we all know, and so by popular demand the officers of the Eastern Division have decided to open the York show to the general public, starting with the April 2017 meet (Friday April 28th and Saturday April 29th).

Open admission for those two days will be limited to the Orange and Purple dealer halls and the Black exhibit hall where modular displays can be enjoyed.

The Orange Hall, which is the largest and most spectacular at the show, includes approximately 150 tables and more than 50 separate booths. Visitors will have fun walking through the aisles and looking at the old and new trains presented by dealers from every part of the country. Nearby they'll see the booths set up by Atlas, Bachmann, Lionel, MTH, and other manufacturers to showcase new products.

As important are the publishers in the Orange Hall. Your favorites from *Classic Toy Trains* will be there to answer questions and listen to your concerns. You can meet the editors and talk about CTT.

The cost for members of the public to attend the show is $14 per family for a single-day admission (Friday or Saturday). Attending both days will have a fee of $20 per family. The show will operate Friday from 9:00 a.m. to 6:30 p.m. EST and Saturday from 9:00 a.m. to 4:00 p.m. EST. Plenty of time to see everything!

This change offers everyone the opportunity to attend the best toy train show in the world. Anyone there will, of course, be able to join the TCA and thereby gain admittance to all the halls still reserved for only members for all three days.

The Eastern Division should be congratulated for taking a major step in opening the model train hobby to new people. I look forward to welcoming all the folks who come to York for the very first time at my tables in the Orange Hall.

Christmas comes three times a year for me: December 25 and the two York shows. At last, all of you have the chance to celebrate Christmas three times a year, too. So bring the family and enjoy the greatest hobby on earth at the greatest show on earth.

Keep searchin'

WHO READS THE "VIEWS?"
NOTHING IS MORE IMPORTANT THAN HEARING FROM YOU

EVER NOTICE HOW MEMBERS OF a band react when couples get up to dance to their songs? The musicians smile, nod to each other, and thank the dancers. Why? Because people who express themselves enjoy the responses from the folks listening or watching them.

I'm the same way. As much as I enjoy sharing my opinions of the toy train hobby and reminiscing about the past in Views From The Underground, I really appreciate hearing from the hobbyists who read my column in *Classic Toy Trains*.

Fortunately for me, I get a lot and lots of feedback. Honestly, I cannot overestimate the value and importance of the various responses sent by readers. They let me know that what I am writing is reaching and touching hobbyists.

I don't care whether the feedback is positive or negative – although you can guess which type I prefer! Different responses to what my friends jokingly call "Views According to Lou" show folks are reading my columns and being stimulated to think about my ideas about the best hobby in the world.

Feedback comes from different sources. People who stop by my Underground Railroad Shoppe enjoy voicing their opinions and suggesting topics for future columns. So do all the guys I meet at train shows, including the semi-annual meets held by the Eastern Division of the Train Collectors Association in York, Pa.

Who are these readers of my column who want to tell me what they think? Most of them are men over 55 years of age. Some, though not a majority, belong to the TCA and other collecting or operating clubs and organizations.

I'm pleased to say hobbyists commenting in person, over the phone, by letter, or via email come from all over the world. I've gotten responses from people living in every part of the U.S., along with Canada, England, France, Germany, and the Netherlands. One fellow from Australia even sends me a railroad calendar each year featuring photos of trains from Down Under. I'm grateful to this reader, who prefers to contact me anonymously.

My favorite story is about Ricardo Sasso, who lives in Brazil. He has been reading my column and subscribing to *Classic Toy Trains* for many years. Three years ago Ricardo and three of his friends appeared at my table at the York show. I was pleased to meet this group from Brazil. We took photos and had fun exchanging stories. Ricardo and his friends from Brazil said they would share experiences with the group of train enthusiasts that meets back at home.

Ricardo has continued to travel to Pennsylvania for the York shows. Flying from South America shows the depth of his commitment to our hobby. This past Christmas, Ricardo sent photos of his O gauge layout and his family, proof the toy train hobby is flourishing far from our shores.

Let me close by stating that I read and think about every letter and email I receive. I acknowledge every email but just aren't able to answer every letter. But I am very grateful to everyone who takes the time to write and share thoughts.

If the quantity and quality of responses I get to my columns gives an accurate picture of the interest in this hobby, I am happy to say the hobby is alive and well. You readers are part of my life, and I write Views From The Underground for you, always aiming to inform and entertain.

Perry Como used to say at the end of his TV show, "Keep those cards and letters coming." I agree but just want to expand the message, "Keep those cards and letters and emails coming." What you write might inspire the next column.

Keep searchin'

GRANDDADS & NEW DADS
DIFFERENT GENERATIONS STILL WANT TOY TRAINS

PERSONAL EXPERIENCE—BACKED UP BY what my accountant tells me—shows I sell about the same quantity of train sets and individual items every holiday season. So the amounts don't change. But the people buying continue to be different.

I do have many regular customers at the Underground Railroad Shoppe. These terrific folks have been purchasing new and vintage trains from me throughout the 31 years I've been in business. I value the people who return year after year, but I pay special attention to new faces – individuals and families who walk into my store for the very first time.

Many new customers are drawn to the store by the O gauge layout I open to the public from November to January. The variety of products amazes them.

The ranks of potential customers are filled with granddads. They're quick to tell me they've come to look for a train set.

Why do these men, most of whom have recently retired, want an electric train? They believe it will lure their grandchildren to visit them. Anything grandpa wants is okay with grandma, as long as it's for the kids.

Once I start talking with the granddads, I realize they're interested in picking up a hobby to fill the free time that comes with retirement. Some of them not only played with American Flyer or Lionel trains when they were young but they managed to keep those classics. It comes as no surprise when they bring in their postwar locomotives or accessories to be repaired. They want to run the old trains with the new set they bought.

Granddads aren't the only group of newcomers flocking to my store. I see lots of recently married couples. They come looking for a train to operate under their Christmas tree. Traditions like that never lose their popularity or meaning.

Once those young families grow accustomed to the magic of an electric train at the holidays, it's a solid bet they'll want another one once their first child arrives. Many times the boy or girl is still in diapers, but these new dads insist on getting started early in the hobby. It's much like what happened in postwar days.

The excitement in the eyes of the new dad is evident. I think the train is for him. Mom also is happy with this purchase.

I steer the granddads and new dads to ready-to-run (RTR) sets from Lionel and MTH. These trains sell consistently at the holidays. They typically include a locomotive, three or four railcars, a circle of three-rail track, and a transformer. Everything comes in a colorful set box.

Lionel offers a LionChief remote-control system in all its new RTR sets. MTH also packs a remote system with its RTR sets, so there's no way a customer can go wrong. Both companies continue to upgrade their trains, helping to boost sales and bring more granddads and new dads into the hobby.

Best of all, at least from the view of a retailer, new customers may develop into longtime customers. They go on making purchases, as they enlarge their layouts for themselves and others. More trains and track, structures and scenery materials, accessories and lights become essential

Sets and catalogs showing them promote the hobby. If someone is thinking about a new train, I make sure he or she goes home with a new catalog from Lionel or MTH. People still like to leaf through them, the way we loved to with what we called "wish books" when growing up.

Imagining what you'll buy next is almost as good as running a new train. Whether you're a granddad or a new dad, the toy train hobby is waiting for you.

Keep searchin'

SEPTEMBER

HOLY SMOKE!
PUFFS OF PRAISE FOR THE GREATEST POSTWAR INNOVATION

WANT TO KNOW THE BIGGEST and most significant difference between the electric trains made and sold in the U.S. before World War II and all the O and S gauge beauties produced after peace returned in 1945? Of course you do!

In my opinion the main difference was the invention of reliable smoke mechanisms successfully installed on the locomotives made during the postwar years.

Smoke was a novelty for me and all the other kids introduced to trains in the late 1940s. It brought life to my Flyer set, impressing everyone who watched it.

Nowadays, many customers walking into my store are eager to reminisce about the toy trains from their past. I can predict how people of a certain age will remember with ease the puffing smoke emitted from steam locomotives manufactured after 1945.

Lionel enthusiasts recall putting "little pills" into the smokestack of their 2-6-2 or 4-6-4 locomotives. Flyer guys talk about the liquid that made it possible for smoke to come billowing from S gauge Atlantics, Pacifics, and other steamers.

Funny thing—even a lot of individuals who played with an American Flyer set in the 1940s and '50s somehow remember putting tiny pills in the stacks of their steamers. We all know American Flyer engines did not use pellets. Instead, smoke was produced by squeezing oil from a red plastic capsule into a small funnel placed into the smokestack.

I never press customers about cases of mistaken identity. Instead, I figure someone else in their family—a cousin or older brother—or a kid in their neighborhood let them play with a Lionel steam engine.

But S gaugers shouldn't fret. American Flyer trains smoked better than the Lionel engines my buddies had. Besides smoke, the early Flyer trains were the first to have "choo-choo" sound incorporated into the smoke unit. Units with synchronized puffing and choo-choo sound showed that Gilbert was ahead of its time.

Looking at the current scene makes it clear trains produced now depend on smoke units more than ever. Every engine, even replicas of diesels, features smoke. They use fluid and not pills to get smoke pouring from their stacks. Different smoke units remain on the market today, being produced by several firms. Experience has taught me some of those mechanisms work better than others. Yet they are essential to people of all ages looking at locomotives to buy. Engines that smoke poorly tend to be rejected by potential buyers.

By the way, the most common reason a smoke mechanism fails to work well is still the obvious one. Someone puts way too much smoke fluid into the unit. Fortunately, once the problem has been solved, the unit will again function as expected.

A few other observations. First, locomotives with synchronized puffing sounds typically depend on fan-driven smoke units for the effects. Second, the whistles often shoot a blast of smoke when activated on high-end steamers.

Firms making smoke fluids are thriving, and I sell more smoke fluid now than in the past. In fact, a zillion scents must be available. I don't like to carry too many of them because it takes an hour for someone to decide which one they like best. My favorite remains the cedar smell of the Flyer smoke because it never fails to remind me of Christmas morning long ago when I played with my Flyer trains.

And how many of you know there is also a scent on the market today that's supposed to be non-scented smoke? Somebody, please explain that one to me!

Keep searchin'

WE CHOOSE TO REMEMBER
COMING HOME CAN BE MORE COMPLICATED
THAN YOU FIRST THINK

EVER SINCE I PUBLISHED MY book of columns in 2012, readers have asked when my second book will be out. So I started thinking about toy trains and the different individuals who enjoy them. Now I'm writing a new book related to what so many of us consider the world's greatest hobby.

If you read "Views From the Underground," you know I use the 1950s as a base for many of my memories about toy trains. Like many of you, I grew up during the 1950s. We think of the good old days when we recollect these great memories. An easy way to categorize these memories is by calling them nostalgia. Did you know the word "nostalgia" is derived from a Greek word meaning "coming home?" Fits perfectly. Many of us feel like we're coming home when we return to these old feelings.

We collect old cars, jukeboxes, comic books, and trains. We love anything that brings back these feelings of happiness.

My book will recall what it was like to grow up in the 1950s. It will also consider how our diverse experiences back then made us the kind of folks we are today. We remember things that recall those feelings. Feelings of happiness come alive when we operate vintage toy trains, watch old TV shows and movies, sit behind the wheel of an old car, and dance to tunes from the early days of rock 'n' roll.

The flip side of the nostalgia coin is that we choose to forget many of the things that weren't so good during those times. We want to come home to the best.

Let's be honest. The 1950s had its share of scary things. A big fear was polio. Every child was constantly warned of the dangers of that disease. Many youngsters suffered and were crippled.

People across the U.S. breathed a sigh of relief in 1952, when Dr. Jonas Salk of Pittsburgh, Pa., developed a vaccine to prevent that horrible disease.

During the 1950s, Americans worried about the possibility of a communist takeover. There was a fear and distrust of strangers that still bothers me.

Tied to warnings about the Soviet enemy were fears of a nuclear attack that could destroy our country. Some families constructed bomb shelters in case of an attack. Kids were constantly reminded of that possibility and even practiced bomb drills in school. When a loud siren was heard, we had to scurry under our desks for protection.

The economy was not that great during the recession that hit the U.S. in the late 1950s. Many of my friends had to rely on surplus food distributed by the government to supplement their families' lack of income. We used the surplus powdered milk to line our baseball fields. The surplus cheddar made terrific grilled cheese sandwiches.

There were many things in the 1950s that we choose to forget—and plenty more we enjoy remembering. We love reminiscing about those days with peers and telling stories to our grandchildren.

My new book will be titled, *Back In the Day: I Still Haven't Met a Train I Didn't Like.* It will review the 1950s and everything I experienced growing up.

In the pages of my new book I plan to celebrate the good times without overlooking a few of the bad times of those years. Especially the best of times during those wonderful Christmas holidays we spent with our families and played with our toy trains around the Christmas tree.

This sense of coming home is what all of us long for when we indulge in the nostalgic feelings that help us relax during trying times. This is why we always…

Keep searchin'

NOVEMBER

HOW TIME FLIES

10 YEARS OF "VIEWS FROM THE UNDERGROUND"

MANY KUDOS ARE TO BE given to Kalmbach Publishing Co. and the staff of *Classic Toy Trains* magazine on their 30th anniversary. I'm happy because I have been a part of CTT for exactly 10 years. That's right—a full decade has passed since I submitted the first of almost 100 "Views From The Underground."

Let's go back 30 years, so I can share memories about CTT. I remember how excited I was when Kalmbach introduced *Classic Toy Trains* in the fall of 1987. Then I was subscribing to another Kalmbach publication, *Model Railroader*. That was the only source I had to read about O and S gauge trains.

Model Railroader featured mostly HO scale trains back then. However, people in the hobby, including me, realized there was a growing interest in O and S gauge.

I started selling trains through the mail using the Model Railroader classified advertising section. I inserted an ad stating I had Lionel and American Flyer for sale. Anybody who was interested in what I had should send a stamped, self-addressed envelope, and I would mail a list of the trains for sale. I transferred that ad to *Classic Toy Trains* once it had started publication.

I was buying a lot of used trains in the late 1970s and early '80s. I heard about them mainly by advertising in the local newspapers in and around Youngstown, Ohio, and Pittsburgh, Pa.

The telephone would ring off the wall, and I would go out daily to buy trains people wanted to, as they said, "get rid of." By doing them a favor, I ended up amassing a large inventory of postwar and prewar Lionel and American Flyer.

With the help of my daughter, Kelly, then in 10th grade, I was able to make a monthly list of everything for sale. Eventually, I bought a used computer that relied on floppy disks (remember those?). With Kelly's help I used a computer—a primitive one by today's standards—to streamline my sales. We prepared an up-to-date list of what was sale and organized the trains in stock.

The requests for lists poured in daily. Thanks to that computer, I could input new acquisitions and delete descriptions of what was sold. Kelly and I could do so quickly, which meant the list stayed current to minimize frustrations.

I sold a lot of trains with the help of the classified ads in MR and CTT. Needless to say, things were a lot different 30 years ago. Today, the buying of vintage and new trains has changed. The selling has definitely changed! Do I hear eBay?

November of 2017 marks another milestone. It has been 10 years since I wrote the first "Views From The Underground" for CTT. It started as a monthly column we had hoped to write for one year. After all, how much can anyone write about toy trains? To be on the safe side, I told the editorial staff that I would write columns as long as I had enough material. Well, I'm still going strong after a decade and have no plan to quit. I have plenty of ideas, experiences, and opinions to share.

I have met hundreds of train collectors through this column. I get to know some by attending regional and national train shows. Others visit my store in New Castle, Pa. Dozens of others send emails or call me to comment on what I write.

It has been a pleasure to share all my "Views" about this great hobby. I love to talk to collectors because they give me a new slant on many of my old stories.

You keep reading, and I'll keep writing about the world's greatest hobby.

Keep searchin'

HOLIDAYS ARE HERE
THE BEST TIME FOR TOY TRAINS FINALLY ARRIVES

CAN YOU BELIEVE IT? HERE it is, the end of August, and I am writing my column for the December issue of *Classic Toy Trains*. Sunshine and clear skies outside, and I have to imagine snow on the ground and icicles hanging from the eaves. The reason for thinking about winter late in the summer is that magazines have to stay way ahead of the game. How else will you CTT readers get your latest copy in a timely fashion?

Luckily, after more than 10 years of writing "Views From The Underground" for CTT, it isn't a problem to shift my mental gears into the holiday mode.

To me, the holiday season starts in November, just as Halloween comes to a scary end and I need to flip the page of my monthly calendar over once more. November turns a page to that new and enjoyable state of mind we experience, regardless of our age or background, during the holiday season.

Of course, a big part of the holiday experience now and when I was growing up in the 1950s, involves bringing our toy trains, including track and a transformer, down from the attic. We had reluctantly put them away and kept them stored for the past nine months.

Seeing new life was the 4 x 8 sheet of plywood we called the "train board." We brought it to the cellar from its storage place in our garage. It served as the foundation for the layout we built every year under our Christmas tree. We gave the board a new coat of paint so it looked great with my American Flyer trains.

In addition, we had to perform all the necessary maintenance to the S gauge engines and cars so they ran smoothly. Then we had to assemble the buildings.

We didn't have much room for a permanent layout. We set the board on sawhorses in the basement while we worked on it, cleaning the track and wiring the lighted buildings and accessories.

The cellar became crowded with the layout. Everybody complained for the few weeks prior to its move to the living room floor after we bought our Christmas tree.

People who, like my family, had come from Italy used the cellar like a second home. We had a kitchen there and never used the kitchen on the first floor, except for company and holidays. I never understood that. Anyway, because things got crowded downstairs, folks would get impatient and ask, "When are you moving that table?" I think that's why they invented the phrase, "What are you waiting for, Christmas?"

I will be adding these types of stories to my new book, Back in the Day: I Still Haven't Met a Train I Didn't Like. Look for it sometime in 2018.

I loved my Christmas layout. Usually I would keep the trains up until the end of January. Sometimes the tree was removed earlier because, as we all remember, it would eventually dry up.

Everything I added to the layout, no matter if it was a Plasticville building or a Flyer accessory, was a big deal to me. I spent countless hours for six weeks in a fantasy land under that tree. Then it was time to pack everything up till next year.

Our black-and-white TV was also in the living room. Watching holiday movies was fun because I was in my make-believe land of the American Flyer village.

I guess in the end it really isn't difficult to think of Christmas in August when you have so many great memories. I invite you to share your memories of toy trains at the holiday season with CTT.

Best wishes for a Merry Christmas and Happy Holidays.

Keep searchin'

PART 2:
I Still Haven't Met a Train I Didn't Like

ESSAYS FROM 2018

A TIME TO EVERY PURPOSE
THE VALUE OF AN INVENTORY AND INSURANCE

TO EVERYTHING THERE IS A season, and a time to every purpose under heaven." These are the opening lyrics of one of my favorite songs, Turn, Turn, Turn, recorded by The Byrds in 1965.

The holiday season has arrived at last—the best time of the year for toy train hobbyists. At the beginning of every year I'm reminded of that tune, which folk singer Pete Seeger based on words found in the Book of Ecclesiastes in the Bible.

Seeing the calendar change and January open has a similar effect on me as hearing Turn, Turn, Turn. It serves as a reminder to regroup and plan for the coming year.

The top priority for every toy train enthusiast involves making a complete inventory of every item in his or her collection. Following through on this necessary if challenging task will guarantee peace of mind and help your family.

Why am I adamant about a detailed inventory of every piece in your collection? Because doing so is the critical step leading to properly insuring a collection. Without adequately protecting your trains, you put yourself and family at risk.

Anyone who is doubting the wisdom of my advice or procrastinating about making an inventory and getting adequate insurance should listen to what happened to a customer of mine.

This individual had spent years assembling a large collection of "high-end" sets and locomotives from the postwar era. Most of the items were in like-new or mint condition and came with their original boxes. Naturally, he enjoyed displaying what he had worked to collect. Shelves filled the walls of his train room and elsewhere in the home.

This gentleman's home had a large crawl space under a first-floor addition that was accessible from the basement. He carefully insulated that space. He went out of his way to limit moisture and heat. He knew this area had to be perfectly climate controlled.

This was where he "safely" stored all the original boxes from his collection.

Months passed before he returned to the storage space to check on the boxes. He opened the door and found a moldy, wet, sopping mess of ruined cardboard!

The cardboard boxes were so wet and moldy, this collector told me, many had to be scooped out of the storage area and placed in plastic bags for removal.

Turns out a refrigerator equipped with an ice maker on the first floor used a water supply line located along the top of the storage space. The line had developed pinhole leak and sprayed a fine mist over the area before it finally was discovered.

Luckily, the collector had insurance for his train collection. His only concern was figuring out how to determine the value of the dozens of destroyed boxes.

I got to work helping him—and that wasn't an easy task. Boxes for like-new to mint trains vary in value. There's no price list. We had to research all the items.

Between the two of us we managed to come up with an itemized list and submitted it to his insurance company.

Even though my customer did end up being paid for the loss, he was deeply hurt because many of the boxes were irreplaceable. In fact, his interest in collecting took a big hit. These days, he focuses on collecting newer trains, since they are easier to replace.

Frankly, this was not the first time I had heard of water damage caused by leaking refrigerator lines in a basement. Many people have constructed their O or S gauge layouts there—with skinny water lines going across the ceiling and leading to an upstairs refrigerator. Always check these lines, as it does not take long for an overhead water leak to do extensive damage to various collectibles.

One more tip: even after you have acquired insurance on your trains, remember you need to regularly updated the inventory because prices change. That means the costs of replacing what is in your collection change as well, especially for vintage pieces.

This holiday season is a good time to reflect on the past year and plan for the new one. With planning and care, you can always enjoy the best hobby in the world.

"A time to every purpose."

Happy holidays and keep searchin'.

WHERE HAVE THEY GONE?
REFLECTING ON THE DECLINE OF NEIGHBORHOOD TRAIN SHOPS

I WAS SADDENED TO HEAR of the recent passing of Jimmy Beaumont. Jimmy, in case you have forgotten, was the lead singer for the popular 1950s and '60s rock 'n' roll group, the Skyliners. The Skyliners were one of many groups that hailed from Pittsburgh, Pa. Others, such as the Marcels and the Del-Vikings, were also part of that fabulous Pittsburgh Sound during what many of us consider the golden age of rock.

I was fortunate enough to see the Skyliners perform many times during the past 50 years. They were always one of my favorite singing groups. I sure miss that wonderful sound and regret that it's no longer here to enjoy live. Luckily, we're able to hear the recordings of the Skyliners and so many others.

Something else that's missing in today's landscape is the old school type of train and hobby shops. And believe me, we miss them as much as vintage rock. I remember going into small retail establishments filled with treasures of model trains and accessories from years gone by. It seemed like there once was a train store in every big city neighborhood. By the way, the same was true with record stores!

But now they're gone. I guess the economics of owning and operating a model train store prohibits their existence in abundance here in the 21st century.

During the 1950s and early '60s, though, those places were everywhere. I shopped at many such stores from Pittsburgh to Youngstown, Ohio, all a modest drive from my home in New Castle, Pa. Occasionally, my pals and I would get a ride to one of those cities and spend the day going from train store to train store.

Today, most of the big box hobby centers carry some trains. Of course, they also have items and materials used in hobbies not related to model trains. These retailers try to make everyone happy by offering stuff for every hobby. So it's almost impossible to find many pre-owned and older toy trains.

I try to re-create the feel and atmosphere of an old school type of model train store at my business, The Underground Railroad Shoppe, in New Castle. We buy and sell new and used O and S gauge trains. In addition, we do repairs on the older trains.

There are many challenges involved with running a train store these days. No wonder some businesses that had been around a long time have left the scene. Unlike many of the other surviving train stores around the country, we do not attempt to turn into a full-range hobby shop to supplement the sales during the off-season. Keep in mind that October through January are the busiest months for a train store. After that, from February through September, sales really drop off.

Some of us have made a commitment to being exclusively train stores. It isn't easy. The costs related to having a sizable inventory of new and old trains, along with those tied to renting or maintaining the property, take a large chunk of the operating capital. And someone has to put in long hours behind the counter.

All the same, as the owners of the multi-generation train stores featured in the November 2017 issue of *Classic Toy Trains* explained, all the time and effort are worth it. We meet terrific people and do what we can to boost this hobby.

My advice to CTT readers? Look around in your town for a train store, because it may not be there much longer. Then do whatever you can to support it. Otherwise, it may vanish, taking with it many great memories. And once that store has shut its doors, all you'll be able to do is ask, "Where have they gone?"

Keep searchin'

THE TRAIN I ALWAYS WANTED
WE ALL HAVE OUR DREAM SETS

RECENTLY, I RECEIVED A PHONE call from my good friend and customer, Father Michael Ruthenberg. You may recall from an earlier column that he is a Catholic friar serving in Chicago at the retirement home for the Little Sisters of the Poor.

Father Mike, as I call him, became acquainted with me about 10 years ago, after reading "Views from the Underground" in *Classic Toy Trains*. He's been a customer of my store and a reader who occasionally comments on what I write.

I mentioned Father Mike a few years ago because I thought it was nice he built a layout every year for the sisters to see. The trains are set up in front of a window facing an inside hallway.

It was really neat how many of the sisters would line up in their wheelchairs and watch the trains run for long periods during the holiday season.

Father Mike had called to ask if could get a Lionel no. 2528WS 5-Star General outfit. He told me that he has been looking for that Super O Old West set for many years. It is the set he has dreamed of since it came out in 1959.

Father Mike went on to say that he wanted one of the General train sets back then. However, his father told him that since the family had recently moved they could not spare the extra money to purchase that set for "little Father Mike."

Christmas in 1959 was rough for the Ruthenberg family, and Father Mike had to settle for the train he had already had. But he always wanted to get that set, especially this year because he hoped to run it on this year's layout for the sisters.

After listening to Father Mike, I told him that his phone call must have come through divine intervention. Lionel had recently reintroduced the 5-Star General to its line, and that very day I received my first shipment of the new sets.

I had looked at the sets and determined they were done very well. They featured remote control, with sounds of steam, a whistle, and engineer voices.

Then I started thinking about how, like Father Mike, I had dreamed of getting a particular set when I was a boy in the 1950s. I wanted an American Flyer no. 5002T circus train, which I had seen in the catalog for 1950.

Dad said the train I had would suffice under our Christmas tree and did not think there was room for another train. I knew better, but wasn't going to win that argument. Still, I never stopped wishing for a circus set.

Since I have been avidly collecting trains over the past 30 or so years, I have been fortunate enough to pick up a circus train. In fact, I now have three!

How about you? How many of you reading this column have trains you never received and have always dreamed of owning? Let's hear your stories.

By the way, Father Mike called me back to tell me how pleased he was with his new 5-Star General. He said the sisters loved all the sounds it made. Almost 60 years after first seeing Lionel's Old West set, Father Mike finally got the train he'd dreamed of. Maybe, it's because he kept on searching.

We're never too old to relive the times and the toy trains of our past.

Keep searchin'

ABOUT THE AUTHOR

LOU PALUMBO was born and raised in New Castle, PA, by Italian immigrant parents, and still lives there today with his wife Marcia. He has four children: Todd, Kelly, Michelle, and Melissa. He graduated from Youngstown University in 1967 with a degree in Psychology and Sociology, and was immediately employed by the Pennsylvania Department of Welfare. Lou then served as Executive Director of the Lawrence County Department of Welfare for 28 years until retiring in 2004.

Lou opened The Underground Railroad Shoppe, a model train store, in 1985, and began writing articles and columns for various toy train publications starting in 1987. Since 2007, Lou has been writing a monthly column called "Views from the Underground" for *Classic Toy Trains* Magazine, and is known for his candid and constructive opinions of the toy train hobby, along with his famous "home spun" humor.

Lou is also the author of *I Never Met a Train I Didn't Like*. His writings are both informative and entertaining for all readers.

BOOK OFFER

I Never Met a Train I Didn't Like:
The Art and Enjoyment of Collecting Toy Trains

$12.99 | Available at Amazon
and Barnes&Noble.com

Toy collectors are like a group of fifth graders on a scavenger hunt…

If you notice the expression on the faces of the guys as they walk around a train show or first enter a train store you'll see the excitement and anticipation of a great "find."

I refer to them as fifth graders because that time of life impressed me as an age of innocence, when nothing else was on your mind but what you were searching for. Collectors all but revert to that time of life when they search for a new item for their train world.

This wonderful feeling and sense of care free enthusiasm captures the essence of this book. It includes many stories related to these times of collecting enjoyment and also reminiscent of days gone by, and when all was good with the world and we were all just kids…

Keep Searchin'

Signed copies of Lou's first book can be purchased via
email, snail mail, or phone:
trainplum@yahoo.com
The Underground Railroad Shoppe
1906 Wilmington Road
New Castle, Pa. 16105
(724) 652-4912
$12.99 plus $2.00 shipping

VIDEO OFFER

The Underground Railroad Shoppe

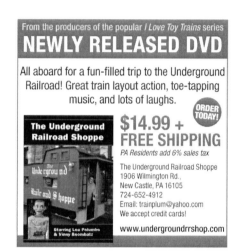
The Underground Railroad video is available! It contains many video shots of the layout and the shop.

In addition, it has new bonus footage of Lou's first American Flyer Christmas tree train.

Lou's video can be purchased via email or phone:

trainplum@yahoo.com
The Underground Railroad Shoppe:
(724) 652-4912
$14.95 Free Shipping

Made in United States
North Haven, CT
30 March 2022

17688546R00109